Max Cottica is not new to writing. He worked with Italian heavy metal magazines for years and had reviews, articles, interviews and his own centrefold published on H/M and Metal Hammer. He humbly started with his own fanzines (SBM, Shout and Undershout) to then upgrade to the national mainstream. He has extensive experience in the heavy metal scene and funnily enough in data and analytics. In the 26 years he has spent in Ireland he made a name for himself in that branch of I.T. with a steady progressing career that started as a data engineer and ended up heading big practices and even play as a Chief Information Officer. Dedicated family man, he has a lot of hobbies beside music, one of them being an avid collector of Silver Age Marvel comics and action figures. In that space he is known as the Irish Spawn.

To Jane, the love of my life.

Max Cottica

AN IT CONTRACTOR LIFE

AUSTIN MACAULEY PUBLISHERS™
LONDON • CAMBRIDGE • NEW YORK • SHARJAH

Copyright © Max Cottica 2023

The right of Max Cottica.to be identified as author of this work has been asserted by the author in accordance with sections 77 and 78 of the Copyright, Designs and Patents Act 1988.

All rights reserved. No part of this publication may be reproduced, stored in a retrieval system, or transmitted in any form or by any means, electronic, mechanical, photocopying, recording, or otherwise, without the prior permission of the publishers.

Any person who commits any unauthorised act in relation to this publication may be liable to criminal prosecution and civil claims for damages.

All of the events in this memoir are true to the best of the author's memory. The views expressed in this memoir are solely those of the author

A CIP catalogue record for this title is available from the British Library.

ISBN 9781035800254 (Paperback)
ISBN 9781035800261 (Hardback)
ISBN 9781035800285 (ePub e-book)
ISBN 9781035800278 (Audiobook)

www.austinmacauley.com

First Published 2023
Austin Macauley Publishers Ltd®
1 Canada Square
Canary Wharf
London
E14 5AA

All companies I worked for and the professionals that were involved in my past as a musician.

Table of Contents

Chapter I: Humble Beginnings	11
Chapter II: Enter the Contractor	17
Chapter III: Government Life	22
Chapter IV: The Years of Insecurity	27
Chapter V: The Great Years	33
Chapter VI: The Years of Uncertainty, Again	39
Chapter VII: Heavy Metal!	45
Chapter VIII: The Next Phase	52
Chapter IX: Here Comes Henker	57
Chapter X: Producing: HATE	66
Chapter XI: Making It with Mad Poltergeist	69
Chapter XII: The Other Love of My Life: ExpiatoriA	75
Chapter XIII: InduRancE	78
Chapter XIV: It Is a Long Way to the Top If You Want to Rock 'n' Roll!	83
Appendix I	86
Appendix II	93
Appendix III	103

Chapter I
Humble Beginnings

I landed in Ireland on the 8th of January 1996. At this point, I and Jane were going out together for the last five years. It was a difficult time, those five years, a lot of goodbyes at airports, a lot of long-distance calls at the time when the internet was just a mirage. My background in IT and data at that point was that I knew how to use a computer and I made reports. Funnily enough, I had that 486 IBM compatible because of a fan club. My father was friends with the manager of Sabrina Salerno and because of my interest in music, he proposed we take over her fan club. Part of the deal was to automate the processing of subscriptions to the fan club and I suggested buying a computer. Little did I know that it was the beginning of a long love story, besides mine with Jane. With this machine, I could write fanzines, I could print labels, I could play games and I could run tabular reports. I could have done many other things of which I did not yet think. So that is how and where I started, in my father's office, in Genoa, where I was born in 1965. I never met Sabrina Salerno officially, I just got a glimpse of her during a meeting, but I knew all her fans. Some crazy letters, some disturbing, but mostly nice letters wishing her the best in her singing career and lots of general love. Fast forward a few years and we go back to my landing in Ireland in 1996.

Without a job but with the love of my life which was the only thing I needed. We both lived in a small apartment in Dame Street, at Rachel's we used to say, a busy part of town but it was not long that was thanks to Jane's job with a bank, we could afford an apartment all for ourselves. We decided to move into this single-bed flat in Bachelor's Walk, right on the quays and opposite the Ha' Penny Bridge. It was exceedingly small, but it was ours. Imagine that in 1996 a one-bedroom apartment in the city centre set you back 42000 pounds. We were renting of course; I think it was 350 pounds per month we paid to the nice land lady. Now we were all set to dream and find me my first job.

Well, there was a problem, a noticeably big one; I had no to little English knowledge. I still remember my English teacher back in school saying that I was never going to learn a new language when I took my diploma exams. The teacher asked me at the exams, "What is the weather like today?" and I started a rant on the Tudors and Henry the Eight. Suffice to say, I did not score well in that oral exam, but I got my diploma, nonetheless. But that is material maybe for another time and book? So how do you go from zero to hero in a foreign language with minimal skills and the shadow of that failed exam? Simple, buy a TV. I still remember me and Jane going to a TV shop in Dawson Street and buying this Panasonic TV – a little at the time because imagine, our weekly budget for food back then was twenty pounds. There was also the matter of buying a cable subscription, which we did but I do not remember with which provider. Long story short, I sat every day for five months watching soap operas, Oprah, and football games to spice up my language skills. I could then write my first curriculum vitae. There was not much in it, but I distinctively remember all the help that Jane gave me, sending it around to agencies and job places. Meanwhile, there was the matter of buying me a brand-new suit. We picked a place in Grafton Court called Best. Because I was going to pay a little at the time, again, I decided to buy two suits on that day. It took a while but in June of 1996, I got an interview for a job with Visa in their call centre dealing with calls from Italy. I think the office was located at the end of Harcourt Street, maybe they are still there. It was not a tech job by any stretch of the imagination. I just had to pick up the phone and answer some customer queries. At the end of the call, I would take a notepad and write some notes in it for future reference. How did we survive back in the day, I do not know. It was then that I met Angela and Eleonora, we will see them appearing again in the next few pages. I remember a very thin Max, in a suit, walking down Grafton Street with a smile on his face because he got paid his first salary and he was going to blow it in the Sound Cellar, at the bottom of Grafton's. 250 pounds a week they paid me. But it was not the money, it was the feeling of freedom and independence that the little job I had given me in return. That joy did not last very long because one dark day, I got called into my boss's office and I was let go because the business was actually closing. Fear not, it did not take long for me to find a new role. Remember the time the classifieds on a newspaper had a job seeker section? Well, I sent my CV to one of the advertisers, a big square ad, and shortly enough, I got an interview. The job was for Computer Intelligence, at the time a leader in the marketing business. My role was again to pick up the phone and interview Italian company owners about their computers and mainframe setups. Finally, a more technical role. It was

September 1996. I worked for that company for about a year. On the first few days, I remember a room filled with people listening to a company trainer on how to move fast through the forms and ask as many questions as we possibly could. The job was ok, the only thing I did not like much was the commute to Sandyford where the offices were based. It took me almost two hours to get there and over two hours to get back, making this a 12-hour shift really. We were still living in Bachelor's Walk and I still remember getting on bus number seven and sitting down for the long trip. Fortunately, a lot of colleagues picked up the same bus, so the trip was actually more enjoyable than just a long trip on a bus. We did usually sit at the back of the bus, me, Eleonora, Angela, Donatella, Renato, and Jimmy. We laughed a lot maybe because we knew where we were going and let me tell you, it was not a pleasant type of work. In March 1997, I bought a book that in turn changed my life forever. In search of more technical skills to put on my curriculum vitae, I stumbled on a program called the Microsoft Certified Professional. I should add that at that stage, we bought a Gateway computer and a printer to complement my interest in technology. 2200 pounds, in little payments, of course. I still have that computer today and the first TV we bought. On a label inside the computer, it says, 'assembled in June 1996'. All must remember the cow box Gateway computers were coming in. It was such a joy to have a computer again with this strange device called a modem that would connect you to a thing called the internet. During a search on Asking Jeeves or Yahoo, I found that Microsoft program. It was structured in such a way that you would buy official Microsoft books for a specific course, you would then book an exam and attempt to pass it. Simple, I said. The book in question was titled 'Networking Essentials'. So, I started reading the book on the infamous number seven and I learned a lot about networks, client and server, Windows NT, cabling, DHCP, DNS, WINS and how to make it all work together. Going back to my job in Computer Intelligence, the Americans arrived to save the company in June of 1997. The Dublin office was going down the drain, so the Americans set up re-training for everybody and brought in new opportunities to progress in one's career, so I put down my name for an Italian team supervisor role. There were many teams and languages involved in the framework of this company, I worked there for a while, so I said, why not? I eventually got the job and was sent along with other team supervisors to Paris, where the company had their European headquarters, for more training and basic management skill up. When I came back to Dublin, after a horrific flight after eating at an all-can-eat fish restaurant, I found this guy sitting in an office as the head of the Dublin operations. The first thing he told me to my face in our first one-to-one was that he did not like me because we were the same age, and he was balding. The second thing he said was that he did not think I deserved the supervisor position. Nice one. So, I got the message loud and clear and started looking for a new job immediately because surely with this guy my computer intelligence life would have been quite short. In fact, I gave a month's notice on my birthday, after asking Jane of course, but that gentleman only wanted me back to the office one week and then I was free of that horrible boss and job. I then joined Oracle for a month, a small contract dealing with Windows NT 4.0 for the English market. My English was still broken at that point, but I survived four weeks of a very dull job. I found my next role, again, in a newspaper. It was for a company called Digital, a big player in the mainframe and services back in the day. They were hiring by the bulk to fill up contracting positions in what was called the digital contracting services team. I went for the interview with my usual enthusiasm, but they were looking for technical people able to complete a Microsoft program called the Microsoft Certified System Engineer. Six exams on various Microsoft products. After a few questions, it was clear that my technical background was not enough for this role, but I did mention that I read the 'Networking Essentials' book and found it very interesting. Coincidentally, the foundation of the MCSE program was indeed the exam associated with the book I bought six months before. Bingo! I got a call back from Mark, my interviewer, a couple of days later and yes, I got the job.

Chapter II
Enter the Contractor

In October 1997, I started this new role. There were hundreds of contractors like me in a giant room on North Circular Rd. At that time, I started reading the 'Networking Essential' book again and started preparing for three windows NT exams. You had a choice for the other two exams to make the six to become an MCSE. Work in that giant room was minimal. We had the freedom to learn new things and experiment with a lot of cool innovative technologies. That is when I learnt HTML, ASP, and other website programming languages. We were in limbo for what felt like an eternity, waiting to pass our exams, and be sent to proper work. It was back then that I met Halil, who was going to become my friend for a good while. Suddenly, on a summery day in June, they asked me if I wanted to join Microsoft on a short contract dealing with Internet Explorer 4.1 localization and I was incredibly happy to accept. The job was not really satisfying, you basically had to go top to bottom with a series of tests, mark passes and fails and move on to a new module, but it was seriously useful to learn all aspects of browsing, searching and overall scouting the internet. Once done with that project, they sent me to an interview with Ulster Bank as a contractor under Compaq Contracting Services. Story of my life, companies bought by other companies and what is funny, I actually worked for HP (and HPE) down the years, which notoriously and eventually bought Compaq. The giant bought the struggling digital company, but workwise and deal-wise, things remained pretty much the same. The contract with Ulster Bank revealed to be one of the most fun projects I have done in my life. They had to build a contingency site for their headquarters so that if a bomb went off on the quays, they could move to Sandyford and work from there. In Sandyford, they opened the door to a storage area with a lot of old computers and printers and phone systems. My task was to network all these computers and install the software that was deemed necessary to drop the office in the quays and come over here for work continuity. It was during this time that I made friends with Tom, he will reappear later in the story, a very professional system developer, and Eddie with whom I go to Iron Maiden gigs to date (Eddie at an Iron Maiden concert… nothing? Well, it is probably an insider joke). I was very independent; my boss would come over once a week to check on my progress and give me some feedback. In just over a month, I had all those old PCs dismantled, reassembled, cloned with an operating system, and loaded with departmental software, all skilfully placed on desks set up like in a classroom, all aligned and looking great. They were all networked with Windows NT 4.0 which I knew inside and out because of the MCSE exams and the time in my hands during the Internet Explorer 4.1 gig. The server was a cluster that was built by Eddie; he also built a Sybase database server and I distinctly remember going through settings and configurations with my new friend. I fell in love with databases right there and then, it was the summer of 1998. I knew of Oracle and now Sybase but I wanted to specialise in the technology Microsoft had as RDBM system and so I started studying a new set of technologies with SQL

Server, a trade that made a name for myself in the Irish markets. But first, finished and tested the contingency site for Ulster Bank, I was shipped back to Microsoft to work on DLLs for the new upcoming operating system, Windows NT 5.0, later, rebranded Windows 2000. That was another dull assignment; we simply had to unzip some files, check some configuration settings, zip them again and ship them to the operating system assembly line for integration. I used those dull times to study my SQL Server books and I got a few more exams under my belt, ready to find an assignment in that line of work. But first, they shipped me to Telford, England to work on the largest European 16-bit to 32-bit migration for the Inland Revenue. Compaq Contracting Services won a tender from EDS, another large services company, to provide this migration. Later in the years, HP bought EDS but let's wait for that adventure a few chapters, shall we? I remember standing in a packed room when they announced this new contract and, in the end, I was sent to Telford with another two hundred contractors as a Windows NT specialist. Initially, I was very bored. I just sat at my desk for hours with little to nothing to do. But I did not mind that because the pay was exceptionally good, and I could fly back home to my Jane every weekend. All paid for. They were even paying us back the expenses we incurred while in Telford. Before boarding the plane on my way back to Jane, I used to buy VHS tapes to watch over the weekend, tapes that I still have incidentally. The pay was so good that we could then afford our first semi-detached home in Lucan, another trend we were part of without knowing it. Yes, it was far away from the city centre, and from Sandyford, but we could not have been able to afford to buy a house in Dublin city centre at that time. Although having your own house felt incredibly good. We are now in 1999. Back at Telford, I felt hopeless with truly little work, so I took courage and I started discussing opportunities with the people who were actually going on-site to deploy the solution. I did the first couple of implementations and all of a sudden there was a line of managers at my desk with new setups to be done – so many that I could only entertain a portion of them. That was a good sign, it meant my work was good and the managers were noticing me. My actual manager often wondered if I was still working for them because I rarely was at my desk. Halil was also there working with databases and on a couple of occasions, we did perform migrations in a couple of sites in Scotland. I still remember those cold mornings waiting for him to collect me at my hotel, but I had great breakfasts with haggis that strangely acts like a hot bottle in your stomach. We were living in hotels for the vast part of the time. That life was not really great, you would actually hate room service at some point. Towards the end of my time, Compaq moved us all to big houses on the outskirts of Telford and that made a dramatic difference on the morale of the 200 contractors. After the experience in Telford, where I proved myself leaving the desk and going around England to install new servers and clients for the Inland Revenue as part of their migration, I found myself back in Sandyford and back in Microsoft. At this time, the company needed support for their Workspex database, a gigantic set of tables badly put together, built-in SQL Server 6.5, and dying an awfully slow death. They were actually paying employees using this monster. But at least I could work with my new passion, databases. My task was primarily to run reports, but I had proposed that the entire system be upgraded to version 7.0, the version with which I was really comfortable. They even gave me an award for the work I did on Workspex, thanks to my boss Matthew primarily. After that, I was moved to a customer centre providing support to internal clients on a variety of issues like web, SQL Server, and operating systems. It was now well into the turn of the century and although I had a substantial number of colleagues, above all Ronan and Cathal, and my boss, John, I felt a bit out of contact with my personal development and career. The exams were going great, I had upgraded all my MCSE skills into the new Windows 2000 stack of products, but I was not really using those skills although I was dealing with other company challenges that thought me a lot in areas where I had minimal understanding like websites and the like. Still, I was providing help on the SQL Server platform and the gang knew that every SQL Server query needed to go through me but in general, I had a sense of dissatisfaction with the contractor life, always moving work, agencies, locations and not really making any real friends in the process because everything was too short and unpredictable. But help was on the way because one day I got called into my boss's office and was told that Microsoft was cutting down on contractors and they would have to let me go. That was a good thing, for real. It was now the summer of 2001. Another milestone in my private life was obtaining a credit card from the Bank of Ireland and the ability that gave me to buy components to build my very own first computer. Halil helped a lot, he even sold me a 19" big boxy screen and that was a great satisfaction to be able to mess with hard drives, motherboards and memory, and have it all work together. How much of a geek am I?

Chapter III
Government Life

The interview was set in the summer of 2001. My interviewers were Colm, the soon-to-be my boss, and Jim who would become a dear colleague. We went through my CV and then there were some technical questions. The job in question was for a Microsoft SQL Server 7.0 database administrator, a contract for six months. Needless to say, I got renewals of this contract for six and a half years! At that time, SQL version 7.0 was my bread and butter. I mean, I passed all the exams available to the extent that my MCSE had an appendix to it, specialising in SQL Server 7.0. Therefore, the technical questions were easy to answer; some backup and restore questions, a lot of T-SQL questions and the last was possibly the one that got me the job. It was around transactions and settings. After Jim asked me the question, I gave a quick answer, and they were sort of surprised. They ask me if I wanted to think about it a little longer, they then looked at those papers that Jim had in front of him and said that was not the right answer. I asked them to go and check it because I was very sure of my quick answer. So, Jim exited the room that was Colm's office to go and check on my answer. He came back shortly after and said that indeed, I was correct. We all laughed at it in good spirit. And I got the job. The role was for the Local Government Computer Services Board, an entity that was guiding local authorities in computer matters.

The specific was looking after some sort of 100 SQL Server scattered around the country and that was a challenge because you would have had to pick up the car and drive to the authority in question, resolve their problems and then come back for the next call. These servers were running SQL applications that varied from the record of voters in a specific area or region to the GIS system that was their land and planning permissions database. Somctimes you had to stay over a couple of nights, but it was all paid for, so no big deal. My colleagues John and Declan (an acquaintance of mine, who I met in my late Microsoft days; he worked as a DBA in the Sandyford data centres) worked there for years and dreaded the office somewhat. They wanted to go out and visit the local authorities where they made a lot of friends and got the expenses back. I was more pragmatic, every time I went out was a few hours trip back and forth and you are on the road driving on bad roads, increasing somewhat risks and uncertainties. Plus, let's face it, the weather in Ireland is shite, or so they say. Driving under heavy weather was not really my cup of tea. I actually got my driving license just a year or two before that job, so I was not either the best driver. So that let me think a lot and I came up with a product that I called SQLesque. Like SQL, that sort of thing. It was a web-based application built in ASP 2.0. A precursor of SaaS? The only thing I had to do was to create a SQL user on the remote system in question and because of my rights on these systems, I could connect to them remotely without leaving the office. In less than a month, I had all these systems available from a single point of view. I actually created a phone version of it spending a little time learning WAP, Mobilesque. Like mobile, that sort of thing. This completely changed the dynamics of my work. I could, in a single click, look at servers' configurations, SQL jobs, backup and restore settings, server settings and metrics and statistics and more. You could, of course, connect remotely to the server using the like of Remote Desktop, but it would take you hours to browse through the server settings and take notes or screenies of the server itself. I had it all in one tab. And way less car trips. In later versions of SQL Server, Microsoft introduced data management views and that killed my product!

I remember where I was the day planes hit the twin towers in New York. I was at my desk sipping coffee and working remotely on a stubborn server. I was incredibly sad to hear and see all that and I leave it at that. I may mention that Jane and I decided to move to Galway during those six months of the contract. Beautiful new home with space to spare for the visitors, we could not have been any happier. With that move in mind and six months contract, I announced that my time in the LGSB was about to end and wished all my colleagues and authorities all the absolute best in their future endeavours. "Not so fast," said Colm, my boss, the best boss I had to date, so much so that I called him the boss of bosses, like in the Godfather, had something else in mind. He did not terminate my contract but he actually renewed it for a full year and found me an office I could go to in Galway instead. I couldn't be more ecstatic, I mean a lot of concerns less, no need to find a new job and all that. So, once we moved to Galway in May 2002, I then started to go into this remote office. The work did not change. SQLesque was going stronger and better equipped with great functionality so my trips were as low as always and work was going well. It then came a time when we had to upgrade all these one hundred servers to SQL

Server version 2000. The same servers were undergoing upgrades to Windows 2000, and we would come in after a period of system stability to upgrade SQL Server. We worked on the logistics, asked SQLesque for reports on the settings and features of all the servers in the project and divided and conquered the nation with a piece of work that took almost two years to finish. I was bouncing up and down the country, I was looking primarily after the West and Mid-West counties because I was now living in the West of Ireland. I had a couple of trips on the East coast for the larger upgrades so we could share servers and upgrade them quicker. I needed to upgrade my SQLesque as well to support version 2000, a task that did not take me more than a couple of weeks because my jobs were primarily written in T-SQL and that did not change much between the versions. After finishing the upgrade, we started receiving a lot of requests for training and it was there and then that I decided to take inspiration from the books I studied to upgrade my MCSE status to, with SQL Server 2000, and write a few modules that I could use as training material for the local authorities. My boss Colm insisted that the training should be provided in person and possibly at the local authorities' location. I couldn't say no to that and so Max goes on a tour of Ireland to impart wisdom to manage SQL Server 2000. Interestingly, I was now working full-time from home. Colm visited me in Galway at some point to assess the facilities and my home office; after he gave me his consensus, we had lunch. I made him a nice Italian minestrone, he was extremely impressed and had it twice. The tour of Ireland lasted for over a year and a half, and we were now close to 2005 at that point. In the midst of all this, I met Brent and we became fast friends. He is a guru in his area, and we will find him again in this story a bit later. The last two years passed amazingly fast between perfecting SQLesque, visiting some authorities, going to presentations in Dublin and studying for yet another version of SQL Server, version 2005, the one that killed SQLesque. In my last days, I managed a new project in the LGCSB, the build of a Microsoft SQL Server 2005 data warehouse. More to study for as the concept was quite new to me and I discovered all this data modelling work by Inmon and Kimball, fascinating stuff and a trend that would help me for the next few years. So, we were at the beginning of 2007 and the LGCSB started moving away from contractors, so my contract was terminated a few months in. The end of an era as they used to say, a sad goodbye to the best colleagues and the best boss I will probably ever have.

Chapter IV
The Years of Insecurity

After the LGCSB, I found myself in a little bit of a predicament. Although I knew everything there was to know about SQL Server version 7.0 and 2000, I did not have enough work experience with the new 2005 version although I passed all the exams. That version was out for three years. At that point, it was so hard to find work when you only had academic knowledge. Brent (you may remember him) came to the rescue, he mentioned one of my latest colleagues founded his own data services company and had already tendered and won a couple of contracts. So, immediately, I called Eoin to see what was going on. He had a data warehouse green project for the Irish Taxi Regulator which I found very interesting. So, I signed up for that and within a couple of weeks, I met up in Dublin with the people from the regulator to brainstorm. My experience in data warehousing was then limited to the stint I did in the LGCSB, but I was confident I could take this project on. After the meeting, I drove back to Galway and started planning. Once I had a rough idea of what to do, it was time for the Regulator to send the data in for me to model and inject into the bare bones of the data warehouse. The data was coming from different sources like the Regulator itself, the Garda, the car registration office, and other public authorities' sources. The idea was to put the data in a star schema and start querying it. I used SSIS for injection and ETL and SSRS for reporting. The schema was solid, but the data was in a terrible state. Although it was in Excel or CSV format, rows were all over the place, there were headers and footers in them, so I needed to cleanse them to be able to land them in the proper tables. I included the wrangling work in SSIS packages so I could reuse that next time there was new data streaming in. In the end, it took me well over two weeks, but I had all the data I needed, in a good format, in the respective tables. And the problems were only starting. The primary keys of all the tables did not match any other primary keys. It is like each set of data had its own set of keys and managing to join the data sets to one another was going to be a gargantuan effort. I then asked help from the people at the Taxi Regulator, specifically to shed some light on how each data set connected to one another. The answer came in only two weeks later, I was getting paid if I had actual work to perform so the whole set-up started to get on my nerves. While I was working for the Taxi Regulator, I also was looking for another contract. So, I got the answers I needed and started to make connections with my data sets. The results were shocking. It was, as we all suspected, an unregulated and unmitigated mess.

Well, some people are going to get a heart attack when I show my findings. At that point, we were, well, in 2007. I had an interview for another contract with Tom, remember the developer in Ulster Bank? Well, he was head of IT for a lending company called START mortgages and he needed a little help on arrears, a horrible job I know, but I had great ideas on how we could resolve his challenges. The Taxi Regulator gig was not going well in terms of hours and pay, so when they came back to me after a while with more requests and checks, I gave them an absurd time frame for delivery and Eoin pulled the plug on me. You may recall that in 2008, the whole taxi industry was reformed and changed, partially thanks to my work and my small data warehouse. To date, I fear going into a taxi.

The interview with Tom and Richard was very relaxed and pleasant. We were friends after all. Yet, Tom handed me a paper with a lot of SQL Server questions. He never disclosed to me how I did, but I say I aced it. START Mortgages was making a mint in the Irish landing market. It was the best time to get in. Actually, I remember I got in through an agency, in the years one of the best I ever found, Real Time, run by my now friend of ten-plus years, Declan. The rate was awesome and although the job was a bit messy (mostly because of repossessions), I started getting into it straight away. The people at START were all nice. I remember David, a young network engineer, Richard who interviewed me, a top. NET developer and his friend Paul. Nice team and nice company if you ask me. Using SQL Server 2005, I quickly created a data mart where I was processing an endless series of mainframe files that required some massaging but were not at all bad in format. Quickly, we established a backend framework that the. NET developers could pick up and transform into a front-end application that was in turn used by the arrears team to do their job. Better. At that time, I was a resident in Dublin at Brent's place. Tom kept me on even if, at that point, there was nothing really serious to do, such a great guy. And he allowed me to stay at home in Galway most of the time. Meanwhile, SQL Server 2008 was just out, and I played with it to prepare for my exams once again. I finished with START Mortgages in 2009. At that time, I got a call back from the LGCSB. They needed help to prepare for a SQL Server 2005 upgrade of all the systems they had and that I knew so well. I cut a deal that would have me staying in Dublin for three months to gather information about the servers. I mentioned about my intention to stay in Galway one day a week to make my trips up and down the country more separated from one another, which was approved by my new boss. I would have stayed in a hotel down the road for three nights a week and then spend four nights in Galway. Great deal and a great daily rate to boot. On the first day, I met my new boss in his office and the first thing he said to me was that I should not really count on working remotely because, if he had to, he would send me to deliver CDs to a local authority on the day I was supposed to work from Galway. Very well, said I. My reply was that if he did not change his mind, I would have walked out. I gave him till the end of the week to think about it. Meanwhile, I am presented to my colleague; he is Declan again, he never left! He tells me about all these plans for the next three months to visit authorities to gather information about settings, features, backups, plans and details. I said that I already have connected SQLesque to the systems and we could run it and there you go three months of expenses and a huge cost for the company, done in 45 minutes tops. He could not believe it, so I showed him my work and it matched his queries and thirst for settings and details 100%. He asks me to share that information, but I just could not with my boss thinking about my contract. So, we decided to talk about it again on Monday, but my boss decided not to let me work from Galway one day a week, so I said goodbye on the previous Friday and brought three months' worth of work on my laptop with me.

Through Real Time, again, I found my next contract for a company called Pioneer Investments. They needed someone to transform the way there were dealing with digital documents created in SSRS for the vast majority. It was there that I met Sean and Bart, one was my boss and the other was a real SQL Server stack guru. Bart built a very complex system that was feeding SSRS with all the information it needed to render a report. I was struggling somewhat to understand the logic, so I modified the system and the SSRS reporting to be more flexible and be more user-friendly. And self-serve. I then invented the concept of an editor file. It is an Excel spreadsheet that contains information ingested by SSIS packages into a small data mart that in turn renders reports in SSRS. So, the users could easily compile information into these spreadsheets and via a front-end built-in ASP, they could render and print out their reports. Genius! It also served me well in the next project Pioneer had for me, the Key Investor Information Document (KIID). Those in the investment business surely remember this European requirement to basically show to the likes of me, in plain English and on a single two-page document, what a fund is all about if I wanted to invest in it. There were twenty-two languages used by the company and they had hundreds of funds, so this was going to be a heavy lift of work. Automation is your friend in these types of projects. I took my humble report automation data mart, expanded it into what, in the end, was a data warehouse and managed to render over five thousand documents in less than two hours. The tragic story about this assignment was that in February 2011, stressed out by work (I was coding in my sleep, if that ever happened to you), I fell seriously ill and had to abruptly finish my assignment. I was completely burnt out. The doctor diagnosed me with chronic depression and chronic anxiety for which I still take pills today although I am absolutely fine, but it took me a full year to get back to work. In May 2011, to tell you in what state my mind was, I had an interview for Version 1. When I was asked what the difference between UNION and UNION ALL was in T-SQL, I put down the phone, searched for those commands and then called back pretending the line was bad. A self-inflicted humiliation and a company and interviewers that will never know what was going on. But anyway, lesson learnt and a question I ask these days to data engineers as a reminder of my stupidity. SQL Server was until then my thing; I had my version 2008 R2 exams completed in 2011. I actually sat at the SQL Server 2008 R2 Master exams to realise that the version was going to be replaced the following year, so I just had the written exam and passed on the hands-on. So, I was very well prepared to answer the UNION question, it is just that my brain was not there so never, never sit in an interview if you are not in the right place. It just adds frustration on top of frustration.

Chapter V
The Great Years

After this year of forced sabbatical, I come back to the interviews routine and find a role in Hewlett Packard that could fit. SSIS developer for a SQL Server data warehouse, my kind of thing. And in Galway which was a huge plus. The interview was a bit shaky. I mean, I stood still for one year without stressing out about doing any exams or anything related to work, so it stands to reason, but the interviewers, Rena and Anthony, were nonetheless impressed enough that I got the job. They even asked me if I knew my dimensions and facts tables!

I joined the company in March 2012, for what was an initial six-month contract. I found myself in a very similar situation like the one in Telford. Huge numbers of contractors in a very large section of the old HP building in Ballybrit. Nobody was sure what to do and days passed with me going to a lot of meetings without understanding the meaning, value, or anything else. Then one day, Simon, the director of the project, comes to me with a small piece of paper and asks me to contact these people on it. So, I promptly do and one of them was supposed to be my direct manager. We had a quick conversation within a few days, and it emerges that he is leaving the company shortly to enjoy a long-due retirement.

Well, said I, a great opportunity to put my name down for his replacement. CV in hand, I met with Simon within a week and got the role of data warehouse manager. I did not have a team then because people were still trying to understand what was going on. A recurrent topic was 'user stories' so I did a little bit of digging and discovered that the whole team was supposed to do things in 'agile'. To immediately comply, I took an internal course on SAFE (Scaled Agile Framework for the Enterprise) and got myself another title, Agile practitioner. So, at least, I knew what people were talking about and started my journey with a bit more confidence under my belt. My team turned out to be geographically sparse. We had people in China, India, Mexico, the USA, the UK and of course Ireland. That was a challenge per se, but I managed within a month or two to create a solid team responsible for the data modelling side of things. The data warehouse in question was built on SQL Server technologies so I was very comfortable with that and the modelling piece I studied extensively and practised for a good few years, so all jolly and happy, I tackled the new role with a smile on my face. Soon enough that smile was turned around by a colleague who did not recognise my technical authority, those were exactly his words. I did not take it personally, I thought he was just confused as everybody else in his position and those words came out because of fear. My new boss was Gil, a senior manager based in Texas. Within a week of that incident, during an animated online meeting with the individual in question, he manages to piss off Gil and gets fired the following week. Karma, I said. The work went on. My title changes to Head of Data Modelling.

At that time, Hewlett-Packard announced a company split. We are now well into 2013. The data warehouse appeared from nowhere ahead of time and I was taking over the shift from China in the morning and handing over to the Mexicans and the USA colleagues in the evening, making my day over 12 hours long. I had a system. In the morning, I was taking over from China at 6 am in the comfort of my home office. Quick shower then drove to the office where I stayed till 4 pm, then drove back home where I handed over the work to the US shift. Rinse and repeat for another three years without a substantial change. Meanwhile, the data warehouse was migrated to an HP product called Vertica, the ETL work was moved to Informatica, and the team went through a gazillion restructures. And the side of HP I was working on was renamed to Hewlett Packard Enterprise. I remember at that time, Hadoop was taking over the open-source world and I took a course with it at the centre stage of a phenomenon called BIG data. Then rumours started to permeate the office, in a brand-new building just beside the old one, that they were pulling the plug on the enterprise side of HP. I actually drew a doodle of a balloon attached to a brick. The brick was HPE, and the balloon was HP. I also drew a pair of scissors in between. Snap and HP will fly, and its counterpart will fall. Without knowing any better and just in case, I started the never-ending process of finding a new role and stumbled on a fixed-term contract with AIB, a large bank, as a data science manager. Data science, at that time, was just a passion of mine. It fascinates me to date with all this theory that seems to have been written in the Middle Ages and this rediscovery of statistics and maths in an open-source world where computer power and storage were not a challenge anymore. I got the job primarily for my leadership skills because let's face it, I am no PhD nor a data scientist per se, but ultimately Johnathan, the actual head of the practice, just wanted someone to tell his people what to do. Little did I know that Johnathan was going to become the new chief data officer and that I, within three months into the job, was meant to be promoted to head of data science and BIG data solutions. To achieve that, the first thing I did, with the small team I had to manage, was to put them on agile trains. Agile trains are a thing of mine, where people get assigned work and user stories and instead of going on a sprint, they go on a train that takes stops and might stop at someone else's station where the line of work becomes one, sort of speak. These kids (mind you, all PhDs so I use the term kids only because they were younger than me) were so excited! "I cannot help you right now because I am on a train," I heard saying around. After a couple of weeks on trains and given that I told them all the ins and outs of agile development and methodology, the team started producing something very special for the bank, models, and algorithms. We worked together on a variety of bank products, credit cards, accounts, cash, ATMs and internally for groups like HR to take data and look at it through a different lens. I was the glue between business challenges and data science. Initially, I would take that over to the team, later in the journey, I would bring a couple of team members with me, and things really started rolling. Then came the time to increase the team size because we were taking over a lot of work. So, I wrote a job spec to attract talent and people were pouring at the door. Fascinating discussions, improbable ones as well, between the gig and the reels I assembled an avenging team of roughly twenty people. Now we really are in business. We took over all we could really, these kids were thirsty for new projects at all times. There was a major challenge in the way. The kids were spending 70% of their time wrangling and prepping the data they needed to mine. We discussed that with my number two Kevin and he and another group of contractors came up with a solution that would completely change the game in our favour. They leveraged the Hadoop data lake in conjunction with other open-source technologies like Spark, Kafka, and Jenkins to create a framework where data would be ingested and passed through an algorithm-like page-long Scala code and come out cleansed, enriched, and ready to be modelled. Perfect. That was so good that I suggested we enter a competition organised by a company called TDWI (Transforming data with intelligence) in the data management category. We actually won in our category in 2017. The decision was difficult, but I sent Kevin and another colleague to claim the award in California. Retrospectively, I believe it was a great call because they came up with the idea, Kevin wrote all the necessary forms to enter the competition and above all, it was an extended team effort so it would have been very selfish if I had gone to claim the award.

One day towards the end of my contract, my boss came to me with a budget control request to let two members of my team go. I did not obey and let only one go, the other left on his own a bit later. The one that I let go, unfortunately, caused a little bit of chaos with the asset management team. I actually mentioned that in reply to a question during an interview with the Bank of Ireland, they asked me what the thing in my career was that I regretted the most. I thought that example was perfect, but they scored me zero in their notes for the answer I gave. I will never understand that and funnily enough, that is the thing that I regret the most in my career!

Besides that, I had a great time at AIB. I attended lots of events, spoke at others, attended panels and gave keynote speeches. I was really on top of my game, I had a great boss and colleagues and a great team to work with it. I miss it every day.

Chapter VI
The Years of Uncertainty, Again

For six months, Staycity, a company based in Dublin, was after my case. We met a few times, even in a restaurant, and they ultimately offered to basically double my salary in AIB, so I said yes. They were looking for a chief information officer and I bet I won their hearts with a presentation I did during the lengthy interview process, detailing how I would bring the company from zero to hero in the data and analytics space. It was not all about data and analytics. There was a helpdesk, IT, a website, and compliance to GDPR, the infamous European privacy regulation that came into effect in May 2018. My boss used to say that I owned all the processes in the business, but they never officially announced my arrival at the company, so my work was harder from the very start. And of course, there was this three-year data and analytics plan which I never manage to really implement. Within a couple of weeks, I met all the senior leadership in one-to-ones, and I sort of was very satisfied with the outcomes. I had plans for all the facets of the business. Unfortunately, there was the gloom of GDPR and that was where I concentrated all my efforts from day one. Mind you, the exercises I went through whilst assessing the level of compliance for the company were very useful for everything else including my data and analytics plans.

For good measure, I took one item from those plans and decided to implement changes in parallel with my GDPR plans. The company was heavily relying on Excel for their day-to-day tasks and meetings. Huge piles of printouts were circulated before every major meeting, and I could not stand that. I remember calling these meetings 'the Bingo games' because everyone around the table was shouting numbers which at that time did not make any sense to me whatsoever and I just wanted to make an immediate impact on the trail of business transformation. So, I decided to run a proof of concept exercise using several visualization platforms like QlikView and Tableau and Power BI and Looker. I took a single data set from the finance area, and I painstakingly created the same dashboard using all those platforms. Visualization was not my main skill, so it took me some time to complete this exercise. Meanwhile, the news of a brand-new office to move to started to circulate in the corridors. That would have given me an extra opportunity to have an impact on the Bingo meetings and with my head of IT, Peter, we devised a plan to have TVs in all the meeting rooms and connectivity to the company's network to broadcast the weekly numbers. Out of the proof of concept, Power BI was the winner, so now I had to present my findings to the CEO and try to influence him to adopt the new platform for any visualization needs the company may have had. It was an easy affair because my boss copped on all of the advantages the new platform had and he gave me the go-ahead to find a Power BI expert. Meanwhile, I choose a SaaS platform to help me with GDPR compliance, OneTrust, a very smart software that allows you to be hand in hand with the requests of the GDPR program and easy and sustainable solutions to the same demands. I actually had to travel to London to get a certification to use proficiently the platform, which I did, and I passed my exam on the first try.

The choice of a Power BI guru was not that easy. Real Time sent me a copious number of curricula of viable candidates, and I had to make hard choices during the process. I remember I stood up a hands-on test to help me discern between the candidates. I just wanted to see how they tackled a visualization project from the get-go, leaving them a white canvas with some test data I gathered from our customer support team. Incidentally, that was concurrent project number three. I developed a quick Microsoft Access application to support the customer engagement team who would use the same to log interactions with customers. That was not a smart decision on my side because we went through a lot of versions of the application and I would say that from the go live to the last day of my contract that took 20% of my time every day between updates, changes, managing the backend databases, adding features and reporting. Anyway, in the meantime, I made friends with Dan, a very nice guy who gave me one of those looks that kill because I sat on his chair on the first week. Bromance from the get-go. I remember I made other friends Giuseppe, Conor, and Gail. Meanwhile, I went through the interview process for the Power BI developer, back-to-back interviews with probably ten different candidates, single interviews because I respected their time more than mine and after examining closely the results of the test I prepared, one winner was chosen in the person of Ian. A clear winner if you ask me and a great guy to have around. I joined the company in October 2017, and it was now March 2018, two months before the GDPR went live. So, I needed all the help I could get from my colleagues, but you remember I mentioned that the company never really announced the fact that I was hired to take charge of all the business processes? Well, I spent more time telling everybody who I was, never mind, getting help.

A few faithful took ownership of their applications and tasks. The COO of the company came to two meetings and always complained that I was doing too much in the GDPR space. Do not need this, don't need that, so I was left almost alone to deal with a matter that shouldn't have been my primary goal. And when compliance comes into place your work never ends. There are new sites to certify, there are new applications and databases to take onboard and log in to the OneTrust platform, and it was continuous work until I left the company. But before we get to that, I must say, I have a good few other milestones. Power BI eventually replaced Excel and these meetings we had every week turned into useful and meaningful for everybody involved. We hired a data scientist for the summer, Karthik, and I got him to concentrate on two things, a chatbot and predictive analytics. I also decided to outsource the IT helpdesk and that led to cost savings and more interaction between the company that was running that part of the business and the business itself. Meanwhile, Dan joined my team as the front and backend developer for our website and we did great work in the customer experience and SEO space. Then whilst assessing the business for GDPR compliance, I discovered thirty-five different data sources that I was thinking to consolidate into a data warehouse as per my 'year two' strategic plans. In that perspective, I did another proof of value involving Microsoft with Azure, Snowflake and Oracle. Took me a while to adapt to the three different platforms but I ultimately decided to go for Azure because the company was predominantly a Microsoft company. Power BI, Office 365, Dynamics, NAV, Sharepoint, Active Directory… it stood to reason. So, I started writing a paper on how to move our data assets to the cloud; I was thinking of integrators like Talend for the SaaS platforms we owned, to move Power BI to the cloud experience and all those nice things when something did not feel right, again. My experience with the CEO of the company was sort of sweet and sour. On one side, he would light up and have goosebumps when I presented him with a new idea or a new visualization deck, on the other, he was reluctant to give me the budget I needed for the things I wanted to implement. I mean, my first budget meeting lasted 20 seconds and he told me to cut my budget in half when I was very careful to just put the stuff, we really needed in it. My second budget meeting was a bit longer but after the CIO office took on other people's projects like SEO or Salesforce, again, he asked me to chop my budget in half without listening to me. I could only do a few things for the company, and I started slacking in terms of attendance and will. I then was again chronically depressed and chronically anxious. My doctor put me back on pills and I was back to where I was nine years before. The bottom line is that one day my CEO invited me to attend a one-to-one outside of the new office to address my request to be able to work from home one day a week and he opened the flood gates. You are not attending work for the hours we pay you for, your mood has changed, your enthusiasm has vanished, what are you doing with your 40 hours a week and the thing that did the most damage, your colleagues are complaining about you. I think I mumbled something about my depression but with little conviction. Two days after that conversation I decided to quit. I knew that I could not go back to that office, after all, he said negatively of me. Mind you, he was absolutely spot on. It is still a blur because I just was not me in those days, but my boss called me into his office where I left my letter of resignation and that is as much as I remember of that conversation. The next three months were very difficult because I just needed to stop and regroup like I did back in 2011, but at least I arrived in the office on time every day and on 7th June 2019, finally, arrived my last day. I said sweet and sour before and I repeat that because that is how I felt with the experience I had in Staycity. A lot of responsibility and accountability and very few knew who and what I was from day one, on the other side I did my best to move the company from the dark ages to a more modern approach towards data and analytics and IT in general. At least, I met Dan who was very supportive throughout and just an overall good friend. I actually, for a split second, decided to retire after that experience but destiny had other plans for my imminent future.

And now let me open a big parenthesis.

Chapter VII
Heavy Metal!

I never knew I had a predisposition for music. I mean when I was a kid, I played the flute in school and although I was able to reproduce classics like the Star Wars theme, for example, I never labelled myself as a musician. I hear you laughing. Yes, because flautists are musicians.

Open the debate.

Earlier on in the years you would find me on a plastic Vespa wearing full scuba gear including a harpoon gun and mask, screaming out of my lungs things like "Let it be, let it beeee" or more appropriate for an Italian "Mi ritorni in mentee, bella come seiiii" or my favourite from Adriano Celentano "Azzurrooo il pomeriggio e' proprio azzurrooo e lungo per meeee…"

I really started listening to music with a strange and tricky box called the radio. I could move a knob and the music would change, I could move a knob and the music would be louder. Gawd, that was witchery! So, it goes that my parents had this black Philips radio, and one day I decided not just to listen to it but see what was inside. Thanks to some research in the kitchen, I found what the adults called a screwdriver. Demonic artefact all together. It would go in a screw, obviously, turn it and crack things open. Well, the inside of the radio was curious. Little tiny things connected to larger things with a strange metallic material and cables everywhere.

That wasn't enough! I thought now that I got this thing open let's see if I can dismantle it and put it back again. So, using the demonic tool, I got rid of all the screws I could find, and I was then left with these tiny little things (I did not know the word component at the time), but I can't use the demonic tool on these. To my astonishment, I realised I could strip them of a green board just using my tiny hands that would go anywhere, so I proceeded to take all these little things apart and place them on the table in order, so I would remember where they would go back in.

The scream of Rita, my mother, is still echoing in my ears today. So, there it is, a perfectly good and expensive for the time radio, dismembered to the tiniest component, yet neatly lined up on the living room table. To my surprise, when I tried to calm her down by saying, "Don't worry, I'll put it back in no time," she sort of looked at me the same way you look at a ball that does not fit into a square (a reference to one of my favourite toys).

The radio was eventually replaced by my father, surely after saving for six months. They then became smarter and allowed me to listen to it only if supervised, so I remember those hot summers stretched on the kitchen table with my parents sitting on the chairs and listening to the latest hits and the glorious successes of the past.

Matter of fact is, I listened to tons of music from a very young age. My parents were class '41 and '42 so I got exposed very soon to what they believed was the real music. Presley, Kelly, Sinatra and the rat-pack, a pinch of Little Richard, a splash of Coltrane. A Spanish omelette, if you will. That said, I loved taking records and putting them on the turntable. Actually, for years and for the 45 RPM only, I used a curious orange box. It was cool, you could get the records in vertically and could bring them around the house, like a prototype of a boom box. I had that gizmo for years, I used it extensively for my collection of kids' fairy tales records, something that was called 'Fiabe Sonore', a series of 45 RPMs accompanied by lovely books to make sure you got the stories right. Ah! The memories. But anyway, going back to the matter under the lens here, those old records my folks had were way cool. Yes, there was the odd 'WTF is this' thrown in for good measure but overall, what they had humbly assembled, I am positive, formed me musically at a very early age.

So, it goes that the parents noticed this attachment of mine to music and singing along so they switched from buying me toys to buying me records and that was fantastic. They made it simple, they went on the Italian top ten for 33s and 45s and bought them all for me. It was more of a Christmas occasion mind you, so I basically played those records for a full year before I could get my chubby yet small hands on some new haulage. But that exercise was also good, I started memorising lyrics and riffs and played them in my head in different tunes or different sequences, fun, fun, fun! Sometimes, I made up songs out of other songs, patching them all together using a turn table and a Philips tape recorder that I remember made me feel I was in a real record studio so sophisticated it was for the time. At this point, we are probably talking about 1974, so nine years of age and goofing around with a lot of records.

I had a great variety of genres on my hands, but it was clear that my favourite was rock in any form or shape. So, I literally consumed records from Suzie Quattro, Elton John, Queen, Elvis Presley and the like but I also appreciated the craftmanship of giants like Barry White, Gary Glitter, Eddie

Olman and many more. One thing that I didn't realise I was missing is listening to bands instead of solo artists. It was a fine line for me because the single artist still has a band in the background, and it was hard for me to distinguish between one and the other. It didn't take long though.

I need to admit, and probably this will horrify those who know me already (I mean down this book you will find out my moniker was 'The Heretic'), but the first real band I started to appreciate as a combo was an Italian band called Pooh. Yes, I know, let's start the laughing choir. Probably, they didn't even realise they called themselves 'shit' but shit they aren't. One of the songs I adored was 'Linda' which I believe came out in late '76. And yes, I jumped a couple of years ahead, otherwise, my project to write a two hundred pages book will take 20 years…

Now I had it, a band is an ensemble where every part is played by a great musician in that role, whilst a solo artist is a great musician who plays with other great musicians, a very distinctive difference. No subtlety here, one is one thing, the other is another thing altogether. Remember that at this stage I was eleven so yes, I knew no prodigy child at that point but still, this was 1976 in Italy, not 1985 on Sunset Boulevard.

So, let's jump another couple of years ahead. Let's jump to what literally changed my life for good. So far, I have been plying records on the curious orange box if forty-fives, the alien-like Philips recorder if there were tapes and a curious 33s and 78s player …

Parenthesis – as part of their collection my parents had inherited, in the years, a good number of 78 RPM records. The format varied from mid-sized to full-sized and they were very heavy. And very fragile and I got a good few scuffs for having broken a couple or maybe more, who knows. This played different things like opera, I loved Carmen and Maria Callas, I adored The Swan Lake and Tchaikovsky but what was really intriguing for me was the theatre comedies and the Duce's speeches. Let's stay calm, one thing at a time. On the theatre comedy records, there was the voice of this Genovese actor named Gilberto Govi. Can you believe that I listened to them so much that I can still quote chunks of them accurately today? They were predominantly recordings from the mid to late fifties, great comedies like 'I Manezzi Pe' Maiâ Na Figgia', 'Colpi di timone', 'Pignasecca e Pignaverde' or my absolute favourite 'Quello buonanima'. I can see the faces of non-Italian speakers melting now as you are not following anymore, right? But I can also see Italians not from Genova melting too because what do you know about Govi, right? Well to both, trust me, this was really funny shit.

The stories varied from the things you did at the time to find a good partner for your only daughter, the life of an ex-boat captain, the turmoil around an inconsolable widow who then discovers the dead husband was cheating on her, to the funny couple discussing an arranged wedding, fantastic. Now I realise, this has nothing to do with music yet is part of my life and this, if you haven't coped with it yet, is a book about my life!

Now, the juicy bit. Did I really say Duce's speeches? Indeed. Now mind you, these recordings might not have been originals but refactored in seventy-eights format but man, were they mind-blowing. Just to start everybody off and shut you up before you say something silly, I am apolitical, so I did not like them for that reason. I like them because it was incredible how a single man could rally up the masses talking completely and utter non-sense. I guess he learned from the other one in Germany, ye like that worked well in the end. Hours of talks about 'Italianicity' as I call it, the fact that the world is out there to be conquered and many other crazy ideas around patriotism, swearing legion to the flag, breaking Greece's kidneys (not joking you) and the lovely relationship we had with a party abroad, up there in Germany: the Nazis.

Fuck me, man, that was the 1940s not too long ago at that time. I asked my father if there were more Benito Mussolini's around because I was scared to meet or to listen to one in person. I didn't want to wear funny hats with pon-pons, ride silly motorcycles and bring around this axe-like thingy called 'il fascio'.

It had to weigh a ton! Giovanni cutely renamed Gio' in the years, my father, reassured me that the Italian government was now clear of bad people and things were jolly. I can't stop laughing after reading that back. End of parenthesis…

…so, I was saying about this record player I got around 76–77 that allowed me to play seventy-eights records (and if this is not clear yet to you, these records would play at a seventy-eight round per minute speed, shame on you). Huge upgrade but that would soon be replaced by something far better.

Honestly, I do not remember if it was a birthday present or a Christmas one. Maybe it was Christmas because I sort of recall we had heavy gear going into the shop, but anyway, the story goes like this, a friend of mine, Stefano, had recently bought a thing so-called a 'stereo'. He went for a Pioneer rack, oh well his parents did for him, so you can understand me, not having one was the end of the world. So, I praised, cried, stomped, stopped eating and all those tantrums a 13-year-old puts up from time to time until my parents cracked and decided to buy me a stereo too.

But my parents, being the people they were, this was going to take research into multiple shops, brands, and prices. So, it goes that a friend of my father worked in a shop in the beautiful Via XX Settembre in Genova, in a shop called Expert. They had a great offer on: you would get an Expert turntable, 2x3 way woofer speakers also Expert and a rack unit, bundled with a Technics stereo rack with a single tape recorder, amplifier, and radio all for a mere 800k lira, basically two months of salary. And we don't buy cash for that very reason. Two years of repayments to bring up the cost to almost one million lire. Remember, this was 1978. Not many kids in Genova had a stereo rack. Of course, I was ecstatic because I saw the potential of that 'beast' and the things I could now do with my records, making new songs, recording compilations, playing tunes on a decent turntable and all that. As I mentioned, this event changed my life completely and opened the next phase.

Funnily enough, I still have that rack, still plays well after all these many years. I managed to pack it up when I moved to Ireland in the mid-nineties along with one thousand records and brought it all with me. I also still have most of the records and on weekends I crack a few vinyl up and re-live those days all over again. With less hair and a belly but still rock and roll in my soul.

Chapter VIII
The Next Phase

And so, the day arrived when the stereo rack was delivered. I was over the moon, absolutely stunned by the lovely smell of new equipment, fantastic and I could see the potential of this. No more moving around from device to device and from microphone to microphone and curios orange record players or ancient 78 rpm devices. I think that in the next couple of days I played all the records that I had, I didn't even go to sleep I was so excited and so amazed by the beauty and efficiency of this new device.

Then a couple of days later I got bored so there started the real crazy Max time. I started buying more records and I can tell you that by 1995 I had 11,000 of them so yes just a tad crazy. So, here we are still in 1978 with this new stereo and me going around the record shops, I didn't even know what to buy, I knew I had a liking for rock but what did I know about rock after all? Not much, so I started asking around, I started making new friends, they started recording my tapes and I played them over and over and over again on my new stereo until probably a couple of years later, I had an idea of what I wanted to buy and listen to.

I had a liking for what were called the 'new romantic bands' like Spandau Ballet and Adam and the Ants, then also Meat Loaf, Black Sabbath, Madness, Y&T, great tunes great vibes all rock in fairness but it wasn't until February 1980 when this happened. I went to this small shop in the small streets of Genova, the name of the shop was Pink Moon and there was this guy, the owner, called Antonio. I really wasn't sure what to buy so, in the end, I asked Antonio what was new, if there was anything that I had to listen to absolutely and I am pretty sure he played games with me and he said, "This is brand-new just came from England, it's a band called Venom."

"Well, can I have a listen?" said I and so, the starting notes of 'Witching Hour' filled my head and in two seconds I was hooked. This wasn't just rock! This was, I don't know, noise, reckless rumours, a car crash, you name it but there was this rawness about it all and as I said, I was hooked right there and then. What I bought that day was just a mini LP, I believe it was called 'Acid Queen'. Then the same band had their first full album coming out just after that, 'Welcome to Hell' and I never looked back. Yes, then I listened to more British bands like Iron Maiden, Saxon, Judas Priest but Venom, they have a special place in my heart and so it goes that my parents started to regret buying me a new stereo because imagine in a small house this diabolical record playing so loud, so loud that was almost impossible listening to it. Still, I was very happy. I was on top of the world and all I wanted was to buy more records which incidentally is something else that my parents started to regret.

So now is probably mid-1980, the number of records grew, doubled by tapes and more tapes, my father had to stop giving me my allowance because he didn't want me to spend all that money on records. My mother was always complaining about the noise. I mean, it is rock, am I supposed to listen to it on two or three? The stereo goes up to eleven!

You can imagine, it was one argument after the other and one day, I just imploded, loaded up all my gear on a Piaggio Ape and fucked off for good. I even got a job and kept going to school like a good boy. It was a sort of 50/50 arrangement. My folks would still pay off my school and book bills, my job would keep up the little place I had and my record habits and no fucking discussion on volumes or times when to listen to rock. The job was part-time, of course, but was enough to score three or four records a week and pay rent, bills, and food, which was enough for me. At that time, I also found alternative ways to make money but that is part of another story. For now, it is sufficient to say that by November 1985, I was the king of rock and roll.

Honestly, I do not know when it started developing in my head but listening to rock is one thing but being rock is another. Great, I listened to Venom, but in fairness, I wanted to be Venom. So, I started to do some research into buying myself an instrument. What though? Can I sing? Can I play the piano, guitar or bass? Triangle maybe? I actually ended up buying a microphone, a bass guitar and a small speaker, a Peavey, I believe it was with a second-hand Gibson, beaten to pulp, but still booming.

And now I started listening less and playing more but it wasn't too long before I realised that wasn't enough. I needed a band.

Entrepreneurial as I am, I started making one with a couple of dudes that were living on my block. The drummer, Tony, was way older than me and Simone, the axe player, but he could keep a rhythm. Simone wasn't that great, but he could keep up with playing some classic riffs like AC/DC, Judas, Maiden – so, there we go, we start pulping and pummelling as if there was no tomorrow. The band name was ThohT, we didn't play any gig or record anything, but we had a cool logo as I was quite the hand when it came to designing stuff and drawing. Unfortunately, the name was a pain in the ass, it definitely played well when drawn but it meant absolutely nothing and looked also like it was misspelled. Genova will never know of us, but we went on for a couple of years maybe more enjoying each other's company, spliffs, beers and goofing around in our denim and leather outfits.

Meanwhile, the records and tapes collection was growing and growing. By 1982, I added to my favourite band's names like Scorpions, Accept, Cirith Ungol, a crushing band from the states called Metallica, ever listened to them? And many more. I don't want this to turn into a list of band names.

One day later that year, when in school, I mentioned to a couple of mates from my class that I played and sang rock tunes with some buddies of mine but wasn't going anywhere and I wanted to start fresh. They looked quite interested and in no time, we formed Fucking Force, don't comment, please. As Fucking Force, I believe we released three demos but there was a problem. None of my mates was able to play instruments and for that reason, I wasn't allowed to play bass because it would sound weird, go and figure, which I didn't mind because it was maybe more important with me sharing times, spliffs, beers and laughter with them than making it in the world of rock and roll. Anyway, the set-up was as follows: Beppe as a percussionist, Attilio at a weird guitar that had only two strings and sounded like a crying baby, my voice and boom-boom made also with voice, Stefano at the back vocals and Francesco I am not even sure what he did, but it was his house, so he was in the band too. We had titles like 'Blow me', 'That cunt of yours', 'Better fuck than die', you get the gist. The sound was horrible, but we were very prolific with lyrics and ideas for song titles so we ended up recording those three demos. I got in touch with Stefano in the last couple of years and there were rumours he still had those tapes, and he could transfer them on CD, but you know how it goes, that never materialised. So, I am also short of any other information related to those recordings which is a bit of a bubu in a life story but feck it, let's move on.

Obviously, I wouldn't be able to stay with Fucking Force that long. My Peavey and Gibson were getting dusty and so was I. At that point, we are well into 1985. I finished school and moved to university paid by my father but that is also another story for another book. Breaking up with Fucking Force was easy, I just told them, "I am out," we had a laugh, spliff, wine and beer and parted like friends. The band then imploded and Genova will never know about them either.

But not all these years were time wasted. I managed to keep up with school, a part-time job, two bands, several habits and I still was young, fresh, very active and things with my folks were getting better after the split so, top of the world as always. Musically speaking, I might not have been a great singer, but I could scream, and shout and the bass skills were getting better by the day apart from the Fucking Force break. So overall, not bad.

Chapter IX
Here Comes Henker

We were actually almost all at the same university, so we kept in touch but the times we were playing together will remain unspoken of, forever. Meanwhile, I started making friends with new people and there was a guy that really helped me out in those years, Alessandro. Not only he was a hard rock connoisseur and not only he recorded for me dozens of tapes of that genre, but he also introduced me to a friend of his, Luca, aka Ozzo la Pera (Oz, the Pear) who apparently was a bass player and had an interest in putting together a fresh band making flaming rock. Alessandro played a bit of guitar, so I really felt that this was going to get somewhere, and we rapidly recruited another Stefano at the drums and started going to a rehearsal room to goof around.

This place was a mess. The room smelled hard of the sweat of the band that was there before probably due to the insulation material on the walls that was there since the same material was invented. The gear was in a state, the drum kit falling apart, very noisy amplifiers, untuned instruments and raucous microphones. Perfect! So, for the starter, we had to decide about the bass player. I love playing bass, but I sacrificed the possibility to be the next Jaco Pastorius in order to get the band going. And that was a good idea because Luca brought with him some riffs we could start working on. I had zip, nada, niet, nulla, nothing.

Huston, we have a problem.

Alessandro was a great guy, I mean he wouldn't say no to anybody, but a good axe player, he wasn't. So, there it goes a bass riff and there was no guitar riff to go with it. So, it was evident from hour one that we needed a new guitarist. Great, and now where do we find one? Thankfully, Stefano had a cousin who played for a while and was looking for a band so, at the next session, we got two new people, Andrea, the new axe man, and a guy we called Ciccio, a friend of Luca's who just came to support his friend, the band and to roll an outstanding amount of spliffs. At that time, you could still smoke in rehearsal rooms and recording studios alike. Just to keep you on your toes with the timeline, we are now in 1986.

The first night together was very positive. Andrea wasn't a monster but could indeed keep up a riff and a couple of solos, Stefano wasn't a monster either, but he beat hard on those drums, Luca wasn't a monster, but he could bring riffs to the table and played them fine. I had no contribution made yet because in fairness, we did not have a song yet and my English was quite poor. Rock in Italian is just fooling yourself. Maybe with some more modern genre that might work, but on a metal rock style type of song where every word is totally understandable, it just doesn't sound rocking. In conclusion, I wasn't a monster either, but we were plenty stoned and everything was jolly.

The next sessions see us bringing together the first song, my first song with a serious band, I titled it 'Run to the deepest hell', a Satanic Hodge podge of sorts where I was screaming about the Lord of Darkness (not Ozzy) taking my soul for some reason. It was hard, fast, crude, very like Venom, so my head was buzzing with joy and so were the other heads, although the stoned part made everything more difficult, like stamina levels -10 after 20 minutes. But it worked, I was playing in a metal band, without a name.

I can't recall exactly the exact session where we found the name of the band. I know it was Luca who proposed Henker (allegedly, it means butcher in German, but I never checked, I just liked its crude sound). So now we are in a band with a song and a name, and we start already talking live shows, groupies and more spliffs and beer.

I guess that worked as a catalyst because, by the end of the year, we had three songs! You don't go that far with three songs in a concert but surely, we could work out recording a demo tape of sorts to get the name of the band out of that disgusting rehearsal room. Meanwhile, we added to the band another guitar player in the form of Marco, very technical, not really a metal head but man, he could play. He brought in fresh riffs and added solos to the songs which was really a gap for us. He also lived in my area, so it was great times getting in and out of the rehearsal room and having somebody to talk to plus, he really is a great and funny guy. I guess we then felt we were ready for a recording.

And so, we did. Our first demo 'Blasphema' came out in early 1987. It was meant to be this three songs mini thing, but I felt it wasn't enough, so I came up with a song with just lyrics, a sort of a long intro I called 'The demon speech', a 3-minute solo on the story of Megiddo, a famous demon apparently, and how he helped Satan reign the underworld. Perfect! This entrepreneurial effort won me the nickname of 'The Heretic' which I like very much to this day. I am no Satanist nor heretic nor bat eater, but you know, in this game of axes and drums, the mystery and provocative background is a must-have.

We recorded the demo at the Nervi Sound studio, practically unknown at that time. The sound engineer never heard heavy metal, so the sound is very polished and neat with a lack of grit and humph but it was our first demo ad we were all very happy with it. During the recordings, we also took the time to add a photo portfolio to the band. Our photographer, who shall remain unnamed simply because I can't remember the name, brought us to a place with some ruins, pretty cool and satanic actually, and shot several pictures which we turned in black and white for even more satanic effect, I have to say that after having done several other photoshoots in the years, those are still gawd damn good photos.

The demo sold relatively well for a basically unknown band, cannot really quantify but we easily were in the hundreds of copies sold nationwide. Of course, the core of our fans was in Genova, but we were really liked in other regions as well. We also started getting reviews, especially on fanzines mainly because mainstream national magazines weren't really that many at the time and even if they were, we belonged to the underground of heavy metal still.

It was now time to book ourselves into some gigs. Easier said than done. Genova was still in the dark ages as far as alternative music went. Italy as a whole was. Yes, by 1987, a lot was happening in the underground, but promoters and bookers would stay away from metal as they felt there was really no fanbase yet. On the contrary, the fanbase was there and was huge! That said, we couldn't find any gigs, so I went to the next phase. I'll organise a gig myself. And so I did, to the surprise of everyone involved. And it was a success. I picked the Albatross theatre as a venue, probably three thousand places there available. Did we have a full house? No, maybe we had eight hundred people there, but I managed to pay off all the bills including the band's which at the time was unheard of and in the years, I still had people reminiscing of that legendary night, second only to another great metal gathering in 1985 of which I will tell you all about in the next chapter. I even brought to Genova for the first time one if not the best metal band at the time, Sabotage from Florence. There was us and also another couple of new coming bands.

Our performance was solid. Sounds were check, passion was check and a couple of our tunes were very catchy, and this satanic aura made us an intriguing combo to follow live.

I remember after the concert, my parents were in awe. They would have never imagined their son would be able to rock that hard, but as I said the performance was solid although my heart skipped a beat when they told me that. It was sort of getting approval and I liked it. We ended up playing another couple of venues after that epic gig and things seem to all go in the right direction for us but that changed rapidly after what I call the 'Henker schism'. We were literally torn apart by the compulsory army service which was the dread of any teenager at that time. One year of nonsense if you ask me, but for people in bands asking the band itself to hold on for a year and especially in the underground was too much really. And off we go finding a replacement for Marco and Stefano. The hard part was really the drum replacement. In fact, we ended up as a four-piece combo in the end, not being able to find somebody to replace the technical prowess of Marco.

At that time, I was going out in the evenings to join a big group of rockers alike in what still are the parks around the main train station in Genova, Brignole. This area will then in the years become legendary for all the great people, motorcycle groups, bands and more who graced that tiny piece of land in the heart of my beloved city. And it was in there that I met Maurizio, who I would be friends with still today. Maury, as we cutely called him, is a great guy, a hard worker in anything he does and a fucking awesome drummer. So, it goes that we started rehearsing again with a new formation and there was an immediate impact from Maury's side, giving us the sound elements we did not have before like double bass drumming, chilling stop and goes and overall, a more solid vibe.

We played a great gig at one of many Festival dell'Unita', a left party politically driven occasion to listen to music, eat sausages and beer, pizza and many other rather scrumptious yet simple regional dishes, and of course, talks from, even at that time, corrupted politicians. I said before I am apolitical, but the venue was great, and we did well so much so that turned into a live demo. It was called 'After the damage hell will raise' which really referred to the band schism and the fact that even with that happening, your friendly Satan worshippers were back. It was a very hot summer day and I presented myself in very short red shorts. Red to blend with the communist party's favourite colour. Not metal at all though, quite ridiculous but what is done is done.

At this point, we are well into 1988, we had a couple of new songs, and we were ready to record our third demo (first in the studio, second live…pay attention for gawd's sake). We picked a new studio this time, Gallo's Home Studios. He was more of a rocker and the sound we got out of him was far superior compared to the first try. We had new songs like 'Kill your friends', 'H.O.M.E.' and 'Legion of dunes' – all sounding crude, to the metal point and rather awesome. The recording went well apart from me catching a cold and giving a performance that was once referred to by a national mag as 'literally vomited over the microphone'. The best review I ever had, if you ask me. That was truly Venom, remember them?

There were funny situations. We had a special guest on the sessions, Enzo or Enzino, bass player of a local band called Hate. Little point to tell you about him right now because the next chapter is all about Hate (no pun intended). But suffice to say, he was a very good friend, and he was there with us. At some stage, Luca found it difficult to play a double tempo on his bass, a part he always struggled with to be fair. So Enzino volunteers to play that part for us, so now we also had the tagline, 'with special guest on bass, Enzo from Hate'. Marketing genius. Enzo also helped me close the demo with a rather silly Jingle Bells reinterpretation.

On the title track 'H.O.M.E' (which actually stands for handling obscenely malodorous entrails, what a catchy title, uh?) after a gigantic riff played by Andrea, I thought of a stop and go where we could have a cockerel do his thing and a shotgun to then kill it. The owner of the studio surname translated in English (Gallo) is actually close to cockerel so there you go, a tribute to the owner, check. That demo was a great success for us, it sold over 1000 copies nationwide, a sort of a record for a humble underground band. It was mixed by us, Gallo and Enrico, a friend I made during the years in Brignole and playing gigs. Do you remember the Albatross concert? He was behind the console. The mixing is quite crude but served the sound of the band perfectly.

It was time now to look into the side of the demo, things like a new photoshoot, merchandise, and the like. Just after we finished recording the demo, Andrea was called for military service so there we were, short of our only guitar player and left in three. We went ahead with the photoshoot anyway. We picked this time an abandoned hotel just beside where I lived, a great place. As a fourth member, we brought with us our friend Alessandro, remember the school guy who introduced me to Luca? He did a great job, looking hard done, metal, looking in the horizon and all that giving us a great photoshoot overall and some mysticism and satanism.

A great perk we got out of this demo, apart from hundreds of reviews this time in fanzines and magazines at the national level alike, was participating in an Italian compilation called 'Lethal Noise' produced by a guy in Florence. I remember going down to Florence with Luca to sign the deal and decide which song to go for. We picked 'Legion of Dunes', an anthemic seven minutes song with more stop and goes than a set of traffic lights and so many reminiscences to different metal sub-genres that you might call that song 'soup' and it would actually be to the point. The compilation sold very well, and we got that extra publicity we needed to call ourselves 'out of the underground'. The problem was, we had no guitar player to go and do gigs with, worst time ever because by the time we would train somebody else, Andrea would be back and maybe we would end up with two guitarists or maybe end up in a car crash of egos... a mess.

Let me paint a picture for you. In 1988, I was running my own fanzine 'Shout', I was writing on the pages of HM, a national metal magazine, I was playing with Henker, Mad Poltergeist, ExpiatoriA and Black Prophecies, I was producing Hate, I was running my own radio show 'Heavy Mass', I was studying, had a permanent job to keep, I was organizing concerts and I think that is fucking enough. I needed probably 12 hours more every day but somehow, I managed to keep all these things alive. Don't worry, all this will be explained to you in one of the chapters ahead. But my point here is, and this, unfortunately, was the demise of Henker, when I saw the band wounded with no guitar player and no prospects to write new material nor to play gigs, I just let it go. I will be forever sorry but the last thing I needed was a heavy weight of responsibilities with no outcomes, considering all I had going on. So, after a few guitar players' tries, came the inevitable day when Henker dissolved, and Genova lost one of their best metal warriors.

Retrospectively, I would have done the same. I have really no regrets in life, well, maybe one which I'll tell you about in another book altogether and that has nothing to do with music. I did not lose friends or anything. We kept very close for one reason or the other, I actually brought Maurizio into Expiatori (all revealed later), saw Luca basically every day and unfortunately, lost Andrea until recent years thanks to Facebook. So overall, not a dramatic schism but I will always love Henker and what we meant to each other and to our fans. A vibe that I couldn't recreate in any other band I played or collaborated with. Probably even if it wasn't my first band, it was my first real love, if you know what I mean.

Well, this was a mouthful of a chapter, time to move on to the next band and story.

Chapter X
Producing: HATE

I met another Luca whilst frequenting the metal crowd in Piazza Brignole. I followed his drumming career with a band called Hate. Luca is a great guy, passionate, a little crazy but fundamentally a good bloke. I remember seeing Hate in a theatre performing, a great night, with them Darkwish and Necrodeath, probably one of the biggest crowds that ever graced a concert of underground bands in Genova. I believe that was in 1985. A few years passed and I and Luca became good friends, meeting up almost every day, talking about music, concerts and how to battle the bigotries towards metal in our city. I also met the other members of the band, Enzino, Dido and Daniele, all good guys with a job but a true passion for metal and I have to say a great band and fan base.

I came to know that they want to enter the studio to release a demo tape and that intrigued me to the point that I offered to produce it for them. There was only one challenge, the money. So lightheaded as I was at the time, I decided to ask my father if he wanted to be remembered as the guy who funded that Hate demo that in turn skyrocketed them to stardom. It was a funny conversation with Gio'. He didn't understand why I would spend that money on another band and not on mine. Very interesting point and I had no answers to that, bar the fact that I really liked Hate and believed they could make it to somewhere at some time. Bottom line, I asked for three million lire and Gio', good-hearted as he was, cut a check and gave it to me.

The band chose the studio, a nice place in the heart of Genova, run by a guy who, in fairness, never heard a metal album in his life, but certainly was a wizard behind the console, Ogno. We started with the bass lines and drums. Took a while because number one, Enzino was in the army compulsory service at that precise moment in time and second, because Luca, yes, a talented drummer but very bad at keeping up with time. Raw power but no finesse. But we passed that obstacle and eventually ended up with a solid set of four songs and bases. The guitar parts did not take that long, the two axemen were very good technically and metrically. The fan part was the voices. We had to wait for Enzino to have time free from the army and the guy presented himself in the studio with no voice left to sing probably due to a cold or something. That was rough to watch and hear and both I and Ogno were not sure that was a good idea to have this guy screeching through the songs. Nonetheless, with few hours left within budget, we got those voice lines done the best we could. I even got myself in with some background vocals in the last song of the demo.

All this done, it was now time for mixing and that took probably more time than the actual recordings. Everybody wanted their part to stand out, a thing that in music is not really possible, that is why we call it mixing. That said, with an inch within the budget, we manage to get this thing ready for promotions and selling out.

All this sounds quite normal and not very interesting, but I have to confess, I had a great time in many moments in my life, but the fun and giggles I had during all this progress are, without a shadow of a doubt, the best I had ever. The guys were all funny, Ogno was a quiet man but with a great sense of humour. There was a phrase we kept repeating, 'Instead of doing rock, go find a job and start a family' that still resonates in my head as if it were still 1988. And the laughter to follow. Amazing times with great people, a lot of beer and the inevitable series of spliffs.

Now, as jolly as this sounds, a few weeks later, the guys decided to split, and I was left with a three million lire set of recordings with no chance of selling or promoting for there was nothing to sell or promote! I am sure, if you ask them, they would put it back to me not being able to leverage these recordings to get them a record contract, but trust me, they split, and I was left naked with a bunch of tapes and short of a lot of money. I should have spent that money on my own band, my old man was right.

Tragically, Daniele committed suicide not too long after, nothing to do with this story but I can bet it was maybe a little a factor that might have contributed to his final act. I then decided that I would never produce a band ever again.

I kept hanging out with Enzino and Luca, there were really no hard feelings about what happened in the end, just a general sense of dissatisfaction but nothing that could come between us as friends. Of course, I haven't seen them in years now, we connect sometimes with Facebook, but those days and these friends in my mind are the best I made in the years, and I miss them dearly. Recently, I heard they are reformed and entering the studio to record very soon. Best of luck, dear friends.

Chapter XI
Making It with Mad Poltergeist

Another encounter in Piazza Brignole. This time it was Chicco and Cristiano. They had a fresh band called Poltergeist and they were looking to replace their singer who, unfortunately, was a slave to the drink at a very young age. My first reaction was, why are you asking me, I am a terrible singer! That said, I couldn't resist and wanted to get on board like I did with everybody else be it bands, radio programs, producing or writing for magazines and fanzines alike. I was thirsty for metal in all its forms. They immediately seemed very good people and I asked if I could come along to one of their rehearsals to meet the band and listen to their craft. A few nights later, they came over to collect me with a Panda car and brought me behind the cemetery of Staglieno in Genova. Little did I know that place would see me coming so many times with so many bands and so many reasons for the next five years. If you didn't know, the cemetery in Staglieno is one of the biggest in Europe. It's absolutely beautiful, the craftmanship on some of the tombs is breathtaking and is a great place for metal pictures! But we'll get to that a bit later.

So, I entered a relatively small room all padded with materials on the walls to make it soundproof. I met with the rest of the band, the two guitarists Alessandro and Franco and the singer. They played thrash metal inspired by the likes of Metallica, Pantera, Testament, Slayer, Forbidden and the like.

Fast songs, raw energy and to me, immediately sounded like they had a lot of potential. It didn't take long before I was there with no singer around, so I tried a few things in the style that was mine at that time. You remember the comment 'literally vomited'? Well, maybe a little bit more refined but that stuff, nonetheless. I remember I tried to sing 'Aces High' by Iron Maiden. Man, I love that song and it was fun to vomit it out for the lads. But I had different ideas for this band. I actually moved into a clean style to give them an edge, a little bit of what Vio-lence sounded like with their eclectic singer.

We had to address a challenge in the fact that there was already a band called Poltergeist in Switzerland. We went through a series of names, but nothing really stuck so we decided as a band to add the word Mad to the name and Mad Poltergeist was born.

All this happened in 1988 and we were all in for a very good few years of success and almost nationwide fame.

We started looking at the songs we had, my plan was to get four pieces down and get them into a recording studio as soon as possible mainly because that style of thrash, known as bay area style, was very popular at the time and I wanted to surf that wave with them. I also progressed in my craft by writing my first concept. The lyrics were all about how gawd turns us all out into puppets and each song talked about situations where the hand of gawd turned things upside down. I also had a title, 'The gambler'. The songs had colourful titles too like 'Harlequin' or 'Your sins will find you out'. In 1989, we entered the studio to record these four songs. We also looked at improving our band logo and giving us a great cover that people would remember. For the logo, Chicco did it all – he really had a talent for design and artistry. For the cover, I choose a fresco that depicted philosophers chatting in what turned out to be the plan Raffaello had for S. Peter's cathedral in Rome. Atheists in a church, perfect! We printed the covers for the demo in a place my father used to print all his marketing material, have to say, they did a great job. We also printed stickers which we would give away to fans and random people alike. Some would also grace pillars, walls, and other buildings around Genova. The demo sold like crazy, and we became quite popular not only in Genova but nationwide and worldwide thanks to tons of fanzine and magazine reviews. We did a lot of interviews as well, a couple of photo shooting sessions, we made posters and printed photos with logo and address for promotions, we were actually doing it right.

We also did several concerts, in Genova and around Italy. We played in Sardinia once, Ozieri, close to Sassari. We had some covers as part of our stage set. That night we played Mechanix by Megadeth as the second song of the set. The place went absolutely mad. I lost a shoe, Franco's guitar was stolen, beer glasses and people were flying around, so much chaos that the police had to intervene, and they ultimately closed the show which we played for only 10 minutes basically. I then found my shoe and the guitar was returned unarmed. But we did not get paid because we played only the two songs.

In 1990, we received an offer to print our demo as a record by one of Italy's legendary metal gurus, Alberto, the singer, and bass player of Bulldozer who recently had opened a record company. The process was quite easy as we had all recordings done but I wanted to make sure there was an impact going beyond the flashy cover and the venomous songs' content.

At that time, there was a very popular comic doing the rounds, Dylan Dog, which I believe is still going but maybe not as popular as it used to be. At that time, Dylan Dog was selling a little bit under two million copies per monthly issue. So it goes that I got to know and befriend a guy working in Milan for Sergio Bonelli Editore the publishers of Dylan Dog and other great titles like Tex, Zagor and Martin Mystere, very popular stuff back in the day. I managed to get our logo and an article written on that comic and our popularity soared.

I then talked with Sergio Bonelli himself to agree on having Dylan Dog appear in the inner sleeve of our upcoming album to which he agreed with no problems. So now we had a flashy cover, a metal guru printing our album and the most popular comic character at that time on the inner sleeve. Fantastic. You must know that the record is one of the most coveted collector items for Dylan Dog fans today. I still have a few copies and I have received some outrageous offers for them, but I am not going to let them go that easy. To add some interest to this product we added stickers and a poster and a booklet to the work and the sales went mad. We sold out the first one thousand copies in no time and in the years, I got to know that the record was reprinted six times without all the cotillions. So, the real one to collect is the one with all the additions because it would be proof that it was indeed the first print.

Thanks to Sergio Bonelli, we were invited to play the Horror Fest 2 show in Milan. We were supposed to reveal and play the Dylan Dog song, something we worked on in conjunction with Sergio Bonelli Editore for a while now. So, we did but it was a bit of a mess because I forgot the majority of the lyrics but managed to patch it up in one way or the other. That show was probably our most successful gig, we signed a lot of the records after the show and people of all types and creeds enjoyed the night and the show.

And here it comes. The biggest regret I have in life, the biggest chance I had to make it in music and the most devastating thing that ever happened to me. With Sergio Bonelli, we decided to record a 45 RPM with the Dylan Dog song on it and on the B-side another Mad Poltergeist song. If that had ever happened, we would have been quadruple platinum in Italy with one shot considering the comic sold millions of copies at that time. Everything was lined up for recordings and production.

At the same time, we were approached by a producer who wanted to work with us on a new album. We had a few new songs, and we released them as a demo for this producer. I had a Dylan Dog artist draw the cover for us, I had a title for the record 'The Lunatic Asylum' and we actually entered the Ogno studios (remember him?) to set down the drum tracks. That process took so long that the budget went to the roof and our producer pulled out of the project very suddenly. But no worries, we had the Dylan Dog song to record for Sergio Bonelli.

Unfortunately, Franco disappeared. Our most talented asset just decided to bail on us, and it took a while before he actually came back. He suffered from depression, probably all his life and all this pressure probably got to him and had to decompress somehow. So, goodbye dreams of glory, 45 RPM and quadruple platinum record.

In a matter of a month, all of my dreams and the bands were shattered to pieces so small that not even a skilled surgeon would have been able to stitch it all back together.

We played without Franco for a while. The vibe was not there though so that did not last long. And basically, so ingloriously, Mad Poltergeist stopped playing and disappeared into the fog of nothingness.

Franco eventually came back. A couple of years later, he would commit suicide and leave a huge gap in our lives. So much talent, a decent bloke, a corrupted mind. A tragedy.

Chapter XII
The Other Love of
My Life: ExpiatoriA

That year I met G.B. who was playing the bass in a band called ExpiatoriA, and Enrico who was also playing the bass in a band called Poltergeist. I decided to play with both after Henker was disbanded because Maurizio had to tragically go and serve in the compulsory military service. Another one. With ExpiatoriA, I helped them on drums which I could barely play but it was fitting them, so I never thought any different. With Poltergeist, which we renamed to Mad Poltergeist to differentiate from a Suisse band with the same name, I played vocals, not the vomited kind, but strong and metal-fitting vocals. Meanwhile, ExpiatoriA finds a new drummer and I moved to play vocals with them too. I also picked up playing the bass guitar again and I joined a black metal band called Black Prophecies with whom I recorded a demo. The next couple of years went by being very busy with all that. We released a demo and an album with Mad Poltergeist and a second demo with ExpiatoriA

In 1990, I, too, had to join the compulsory army service, but they sent me home after a month because of some change in the law so it was not too bad. In 1991, we recorded a new demo with ExpiatoriA titled 'Symphonies of Decomposed Human Flesh' that had a serious impact on the metal underground movement of that time and also, I went national with my writing on the #1 metal magazine in Italy, H/M. So, more busy days were ahead of me but I could not be any happier. In those days, I also produced a demo for a local band called Hate and at that point, I became relatively famous in my community for the time and expertise I had in all that is heavy metal. Then things started to become a bit stale. Mad Poltergeist disbanded, Black Prophecies disappeared into the dark hole where they came from, ExpiatoriA lost their bass player due to yet the compulsory army service, the radio I was working in closed unexpectedly, H/M closed as well and I found myself playing the bass guitar for two bands, one with no name and the other one being the first formation of Sadist, a band that had a tremendous success down the line. With another bass player. As you probably remember in 1991, I also met Jane, so things were shifting and my interest in heavy metal too. Once Sadist disappeared from my life, I started playing the bass guitar with ExpiatoriA and wrote a few songs for them, but things were not the same. I was burnt, possibly depressed for having given so much to Genova and heavy metal and without the prizes, so my focus was more directed to change my life completely and join the love of my life in Ireland. So, 1996 came, I relocated to another country and ExpiatoriA and the band with no name disbanded thereafter. I was very sad back in those days because I did not know my future, but I knew what I left behind and that took a lot of courage. I could have reinvented myself in one shape or the other, instead, I left it all behind, but I was with the love of my life and that had to take precedence. But you may wonder why did I tell you all this? In 2010, I received a call from Massimo the creator and master of ExpiatoriA. We settled to produce a new six tracks demo that I called 'Return to Golgotha' and so we did, and it was a relatively good success. Well, in 2019, after I left Staycity, Massimo called me again and asked me if I want to participate in the reunion of ExpiatoriA, with all the old band, plus a new guitar player called Alex. The news could not have excited me more. I can go back to those days with no regrets about leaving it all behind anymore. It took me some months to get back to a relatively good shape, but I wrote lyrics for eight songs and an intro, and I felt I was back in the game. Unfortunately, things did not go that far because they had a rough schedule in mind for concerts and gigs, three times a month, and with no salary, I could have never gone back and forth three times a month, so I took the hard decision to call it quits. And then COVID hit so it would have never happened anyway. I know they disbanded during 2020 to then resurrect the project again but no one called me again so that is when I decided to call it quits myself and live on with the memories of those years and the sweet and sour taste of a new dream that did not happen.

Chapter XIII
InduRancE

In 2004, after the death of my father, I found myself thirsty for a new music project of sorts. My attempts to find a band in Ireland were not really successful. I picked up this DVD in a store in Galway. Magix professional studio. A complete package to write, play and record your own music. What can go wrong, I said to myself. So, I load the software on my PC and started messing around with it. I settled on a genre that I define as ambient and instrumental. A bizarre name came to mind, InduRancE (not like insurance, more like endurance with an I) and I prepared a bunch of songs that I released as a demo titled, 'Walking Through the Polyhedric Park'. Back in the day, Ozzo (the first Luca in this story) called me polyhedric several times, because of my predisposition to take on many things at the same time and my multi-faceted nature. So why not a celebration of self in my first solo project demo? The album was circulated on some very early social platforms and received just a warm welcome. The style and genre was there but the compositions I recognised were missing finesse and sounded very crude and repetitive. Not to worry though, I had material for another album, my first with that moniker, which I titled, 'Odissea', a reminder of what happened to me during my life to that point in time and the insecurities of what stood ahead of me. Again, the album was not as popular as I wanted it to be, the reviewers thought that it was a good sound and good compositions but too crude and unrefined to bring me any success at that point in time. The only good comments were around the style of compositions which sounded more rock-oriented than ambient. Or so they said. I took that literally and for my next album, Miseria, I crafted a series of more rock-sounding songs that finally got me some credits. The game was about to change though. One of my older friends back in Genova, a fan of Henker and Mad Poltergeist, Federico, had become a popular novel writer in Italy. He said he had a new book, Lettere da Antartica, and was looking for somebody to write a sort of soundtrack for the book that he could pop in the background when he went on tour to promote the book itself. I accepted the challenge and started by reading the book. The atmospheres were gelid, the storylines raw and obsessive. Perfect material for a new album. We released the album at the same time the book came out, I also developed a website where people could buy the book, and we offered the support of the soundtrack for free. In those days, MySpace was very popular as a social platform and Federico did the best he could to promote both the book and the soundtrack on it. Finally, InduRancE was going to go around far more than my limited fanbase and social networking. The book was a success and so was the soundtrack and everybody at this point was happy. It all happened in 2007. After that success, I wanted to make a new album that ended up being a cross between Miseria and the soundtrack score, I titled that soundtrack to the apocalypse and sported a variety of moods and tunes going from straight disco-style songs, to rock, to mellow and ambient. Sometimes, I mixed up all that in songs and the result was a very hectic and unbalanced product but that was my style.

Federico was looking into something else now; he wanted to pick up 100-ish art pieces from his huge network of artists, painters and photographers and wanted to make a video with a supporting song and an album. That project was going to project InduRancE music worldwide with a huge tour that touched even New York, Paris, and Moscow along with yet another Italian tour. As by format now, I released a theme song for the video, made up the video and coded a virtual environment online where fans and users alike were able to browse the art in a virtual museum-like setting. I also had other songs and packaged them all in what we called Visions. The success of this initiative was huge! The artist who collaborated with us, all very talented underground singers, were very happy with the final products, which I also mixed. The painters and photographers whose art was portrayed in the video were also very happy. I and Federico were ecstatic.

In 2009, Federico released the follower to Lettere da Antartica, called Il Bambino del Mai and he asked me to write a soundtrack for it again. This time the tour supporting the book was way bigger than the previous one so I couldn't be any happier. Federico organised a good bunch of singers to interpret my songs and the results were very satisfactory. Once again, we had a website, the music was free, and the tour did very well. In the end, by 2009 had finished, I had two albums done in the same year. Polyhedric and prolific indeed. If you wonder where the second album came from, I also released a composer's cut of Il Bambino del Mai songs, all instrumental and with little differences here and there from the original soundtrack.

On one specific song, I and Federico had a huge disagreement and we parted ways in 2010. In 2010, I released

'Return to Golgotha' with Massimo of ExpiatoriA and I sort of pulled and parked the InduRancE solo project.

It was not long before I actually reopened that door and on 12 December 2012, I published a new album called 'The Dark Side of Negative'. This time, I had an agency behind me, and reviews were pouring in from all around the world. And also, this time it was not ambient anymore, but I went back to my metal roots for an album which had a resounding success.

Strong of that success only two years later, I composed what turned out to be my swan song album, accurately titled, 'Here Comes the End'. I decided to switch agencies and went for the worst professional relationship I ever had with a thief from Italy who got off me a lot of money and in return, he printed flyers! No reviews, no gigs, nothing else but fecking flyers!

At that point, I was completely drained and disillusioned. I honestly thought that 'Here Comes the End' was a far better album than its predecessor. I also made a promo video for it as per the request of the thief from Italy. I have to say that the YouTube stats on it are quite good, but the album did not go anywhere to be listened to and I was very sad about that.

But I always kick back no matter the situation, so I started a brand-new project called 'The Dark', a peculiar comic with a soundtrack to boot! It is a 160 pages story that happens in a place I called the dark. So, you cannot see really anything but comic balloons and dialogue with the odd image photoshopped here and there. The soundtrack saw me coming back to ambient and instrumental. Overall, a very solid effort which I sent to all four corners of the world (for free) and had a very warm welcome from all involved. I then, a few years later, released a short spin-off from that story called Domus where I imagined that a meteor hit the earth and left in orbit only a portion of it. Of course, this work came with a soundtrack, a single 30-minute song called, 'The Light at the End of the Universe'. This work was not really distributed far and wide, I just put it on my website and left it there for free for visitors to enjoy. That was six years ago and InduRancE right now is a mere memory. I recently started composing again probably bored by the pandemic, lockdowns and all that extravaganza, but I sort of have lost my mojo and what came out really pales compared to my past efforts. The only thing I really want to do is to officially publish The Dark comic book, but I have had a problem with it for the past two and a half years; I have no job and things are tight and that opens the doors to the last chapter of my story.

Incidentally, before I end the chapters about my music background, it is worth mentioning that last year I published my first best album entitled 'The Willows of Attymon'. Attymon is a community close to the cattery where we left our two cats, Py and Squeaky Toy, for many years. I really do not know if there are willow trees there but by now you know me: polyhedric, eclectic, heretic!

Chapter XIV
It Is a Long Way to the Top If You Want to Rock 'n' Roll!

Since I left Staycity and reunited with my pals in ExpiatoriA I have struggled to find new employment. I started asking myself what I wanted to do next, and the obvious response was, I wanted to be a chief data and analytics officer! There is only one small problem with that. Those types of positions do not come by very often in Ireland. It is a small country after all and although we pretend, we are advanced in data and analytics, we really are not. I think that in two and a half years of searching, I stumbled on that title only twice. So, I decided to lower my personal target to things like head of a data practice, or director of the same or vice president of analytics, or data and analytics manager. That caused another problem. A lot of job specs for those positions are a variety of products, SaaS, software and programming languages, and a lot of companies require you to have experience at different levels in some or all of them. I then decided to roll up my sleeves and delve into some of them to keep me entertained and spice up my curriculum vitae. I started from Hadoop again as I have not had practice in years, and I lost all the skills I had from the time I spent in HPE. Followed by two courses using Tableau, two courses using Python for data science and a course in PHP (I know, I know…). I also obtained a professional diploma in analytics and artificial intelligence from the Analytics Institute of Ireland, and I successfully certified as a DCAM practitioner, a data management assessment framework created by the EDM Council. I also registered for tons of webinars, online documentation, Udemy courses and whatnot, to reinvent myself and be a more suitable candidate.

I did many interviews in these two and a half years. Three with EY, not enough consulting experience. Three with Gartner, not enough vision experience. Six with Salesforce, not enough experience with the platform. Four with Bank of Ireland, not enough experience with Teradata and Informatica. A huge number of start-ups where they preferred me to have actual experience working with start-ups. Several mid-sized companies where I failed to tick the box for XYZ software knowledge.

To this day, I do not know how I kept composed and relaxed about all those rejections, but two things kept me going, 'Never Surrender' played by Saxon and the fact that between all those opportunities, I only needed one to make me happy. Also, the never-ending support I got from my Jane kept me alive and focused on the matter. So, I kept going and going and going like the Duracell bunny and January 2022 arrived and it was then that I had three opportunities at the same time. I will cut it short and announce that I am going to be the head of data services for a financial company called Pepper! Insisting and never giving up in the end paid off. During this journey, a good friend of mine, Justin, said to me to stick to my guns and not to undervalue my vast experience because the day will come and all the frustration of these two and a half years will fade away. So now, I am looking forward to this new chapter in my life and specifically career. I know that I will do well, health and luck being on my side, and I cannot really wait to start but first, there is a trip to Orlando, Florida to look forward to.

Did I ever tell you of that time when…

Appendix I

This appendix is a compendium of what I missed in the first draft of this book. It is actually a lot, but it would have made the integrity of the book hard to digest, that is how many side projects I was actually involved in back in the day and their funny stories. So, there you go, I append them all at the very end!

InduRancE Singles

Between 2006 and 2011, I released a few singles under the moniker InduRancE. The first was titled 'Life' and it was a very long rave song inspired by something I heard on YouTube, yet obsessive and melancholic like my style really. In 2008, I released the single Japan taken from a song from Miseria which I remastered and changed around. It was meant to be a single dedicated to the earthquake in Japan where I still have many friends. It was linked to a PayPal account that funded a relief campaign for Japan at that time and I raised a good number of doubloons for that cause. Lastly, in memory of my mother's anniversary, I released in 2011 a song called 'A Day to Remember'. It became quite popular at that time for its suspense style with a long intro and the tune from Instruverse in the middle. Instruverse incidentally became a ringtone as well, it is on my phone right now, still.

Black Prophecies

It happens that I bought a lot of records from a shop in Santa Margherita Ligure. The owner was a friend of mine and I remember our long conversations about what was new in the metal world, how we both loved Slayer and stuff like that. He mentioned that he was playing the drums with an obscure band called Black Prophecies and that they were looking for a bass player. I, of course, proposed to try with them because let's face it, I did not have enough on my plate at the time (hahaha). So it goes that the band came to my rehearsal room one night and the leader of the band, Achille, explained to me that they had these four songs and would like to record a demo. "Fine by me," said I, but I added, "let's see if I am a good fit first." I noticed that Achille brought a tape recorder with him, and I thought it was surely because they wanted to record the session and listen to what I did, surely. Well, wrong! That was to record the demo! In fact, we went through the four songs, I did what I could because let's face it, I never heard the songs before and at the end of the session, Achille was quite happy to have his demo tape-recorded. Astonishing. The sound of my bass guitar was all wrong for Black Prophecies. I used to play, and still do, an Ibanez that Jane bought me with her savings back when she was working in Italy, lovely days, mind you. The sound of this Ibanez is closer to Forbidden or Testament – sharp, metallic, and flimsy at the same time. Black Prophecies was playing a mixture of Morbid Angel, Death, and Autopsy-like tunes, not the sound that the bass in those bands sounds like, but hey, he said that he was satisfied and in the matter of a few weeks, the demo was out, and my name was on it. They then recorded a second demo without me but using my rehearsal room again. I think it was

Chicco from Mad Poltergeist who recorded the bass tracks at that time. The same set-up, recorded live with Chicco not having a clue of genre nor any songs but again Achille was completely satisfied with the product. I then lost contact with them, and I do not know if they made anything after that.

Resurrecting Henker

I tried to bring back that band to life around 1992. It was only me and my good friend Claudio playing the guitar. I was on voice and bass duties. We played for months without a drummer although we had Maurizio in the back of our minds. We piled up a lot of songs in a very short amount of time but in the end, Henker was not to see the light of day again. Incidentally, just last year I believe, I tuned into a radio program on Facebook, and they played one of our songs and they labelled Henker as the Italian Venom! Fantastic, I couldn't be any happier.

Fanzines and HM Days

It started just for fun.

Me, Alessandro, and Beppe with the infamous SBM fanzine back in 1986. We printed five copies in my father's office with a gigantic orange photocopier. We brought them to Disco Club in Brignole and we sold out in an hour! So, we made more issues and repeated the same process for another few months. Alessandro was covering hard rock and heavy metal, Beppe was writing reviews about punk rock, and I was concentrating on the dark side of metal, death and black. They then abandoned the project, but I kept going with my own fanzine called Shout. I had a good few issues, all written by hand, and my spread was now nationwide. The sales were going pretty well, demos were coming in the dozens and I took trains all over Italy to interview bands and take pictures which were all appearing on my fanzine. What a fun time! In the years, I then renamed it to Under Shout and was with issue eleven that I got a phone call from Rome from a guy called Vincenzo who offered me a job to write for H/M, at that time the leading national metal magazine. I was thrilled. We started with a few reviews here and there, they then liked my style so much that they gave me four pages in the centre fold of the magazine to talk about Italian bands. It was called Under Shout. They then moved me to interviews and it was then that I met Lemmy from Motorhead, Steve Harris from Iron Maiden and Lars Ulrich from Metallica. The Metallica interview was about their famous black album, and it was so good that they reprinted it on Metal Hammer Europe a few months later. I think I worked there for about three years. I remember once a month taking the train to Rome to meet Vincenzo, Marco and Alessandro, my dear colleagues. And to get my cheque. Those were glorious days and the first time anyone actually paid me to do what I liked most.

Heavy Mass on the Radio

In 1989, I pitched an idea for a radio program to Riccardo, owner of Radio Magic Sound, a local broadcasting channel. I met Riccardo at a party, and we discussed the possibility of the radio taking a more modern approach and maybe playing some metal tunes. The pitch was a success and a few weeks later, I started my radio career which went on for four years. I was not going to get a cheque, but I was going to get an allowance to buy records which fit me perfectly. I designed a sticker and started circulating that and I called the program Heavy Mass more because my first name is Massimo. I am an atheist though. I still remember my colleague passing me the mic in my first attempt to become a radio personality. I chose Deathrider played by Anthrax as the starting tune and little did I know that years later I would still be there flipping records, making interviews with Italian bands, and having a jolly time all around. A few years in, I hired a friend of mine, another Alessandro, to cover for me the more punk side of metal and he brought in great material and records and some of them I bought for the radio because they really rocked. The radio eventually closed doors and Genova would miss my program and the hours of flowing metal from the waves. But as they say, nothing lasts forever.

Sadist

This was a short stint, but I was the first bass player of Sadist. Peso, who I knew from his Necrodeath days, wanted to build up a brand-new band and asked me if I wanted to be the bass player. I, as usual, said yes and again we started rehearsing in my rehearsal room at the back of the cemetery in Genova. I spent so many hours in that rehearsal room for years. I used to go to my father's office in the morning, help him out for what I could and then have lunch with him and the rest of the day, I would spend rehearsing with my many bands. Sadist were the first in line, they liked the wee hours of the afternoon. Then came Claudio with the Henker project. Then came ExpiatoriA, then Mad Poltergeist. At that point, it was a little over 1 am but my shift wouldn't stop there because I was playing with yet another band at the time.

The experience with Sadist was short-lived mainly because I had to drop something to be fully present with the rest. Peso and I remain good friends to this date even if he doesn't play with Sadist anymore and Sadist having become the cult band that they are today.

Candlemass!

For a short period of time, I played with a band with no name, heavily influenced by Queensryche and Crimson Glory. Not my genre but I do also love both of those bands. And no, I did not play with Candlemass. Candlemass was the nickname we affectionately gave to Marco, the drummer in the band because his hairstyle reminded us of Messiah Marcolin's, singer of the Swedish, more famous band. It was very late at night because of their long shifts at work but we formed a good relationship with Aldo, the guitar player, and Marco so much so that we played intensively for a few months. I then decided to quit because let's face it, enough bands were enough bands and I needed some sleep now and then, but they moved on with other band members, always playing at the back of the cemetery and they actually recorded a few demos and played some live gigs. I miss them as friends. Marco is still playing the drums, Aldo, I lost every contact with him.

And there it goes. So, you now have a complete, 360 vision of what was going on in my life back in the day. I miss all my friends, the people I met in the process and actually doing all those things.

And I miss the rehearsal room at the back of the cemetery, in Genova, the other love of my life.

Appendix II

Anecdotes

During my Microsoft years, around 1999/2000, I worked on a project called Workspex. It was a small team to support such an important and large system, mainly comprised of an IIS website and a SQL backend. This system would stay up 24/7 so we had regular shift handovers with the USA. One of the biggest problems we had was that the website would go down very often. The responsibilities around the IIS website fell over to a guy called John. He was a biker, so he would ride his motorbike to work every day. And he was always late.

One morning, he presented himself at 10:30 am completely covered in blood and feathers. He collided with a flock of non-specified birds and kept going until he reached the office. We had shower facilities at the office, but he was so late that he skipped taking a shower and making himself presentable and sat at his desk like nothing was out of place. We did not say anything until he started to rant about the flock and the reason he was that late to the office. We couldn't spare a few laughs as he was going through the gruesome details.

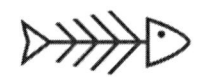

On another day, whilst on the phone with the USA for the usual evening handover, he was asked bluntly why the website of Workspex was down basically all day. He wasn't in the office until 3:00 pm that day. And he came up with a genius answer that I repeat to date when I want to confuse the waters with my boss or something to that degree. "I am recompiling the DLLs," he said. On the other side of the phone, there was silence because nobody really knew what a DLL was and what to do about it. So, Matthew the program manager replied with a tentative, "All right, do you have an ETA for that?" Hilarious.

I was responsible for the SQL backend of the system. One of the major flaws was that it ran over Microsoft SQL Server version 6.5. At that time, my real expertise was in version 7.0 which was a great improvement compared to its predecessor. So, I proposed to undergo an upgrade of the platform to the latest SQL Server version. It was on me anyway and once got approval, I started backing up the whole system and proceeded to install a new instance of SQL Server version 7. All went well although the server wasn't really in great shape, but we had another server we could rely on in case something went down. I then proceeded to restore the database copy I took before the upgrade exercise and apart from a few issues, I now had a fresh version of the database in a brand-new instance. My boss went to the extent of awarding the team a plaque of gratitude for a successful upgrade of Workspex.

Everybody got one bar me, the only guy who was actually involved in the upgrade in the first place. I did not complain, I just let the irony sink in and eventually my boss ordered a new plaque and presented it to me. Eventually. The upgrade happened in 2000, the plaque said 2001. That's how long it took my boss to realise that I was also part of the Workspex team.

While in Telford working for EDS, which subcontracted a huge migration for the Inland Revenue with Compaq Contracting Services, I was at my desk 9 to 5, with little to nothing to do. One evening, just before logging off, I was approached by Mike, an American with a very strong accent. I later figured out that was the overall project program manager. He asked me my name first and I replied Max of course and then he said, "Like my dog!" and I immediately was not impressed. He had a problem with Excel, he saved a file but then lost it for some reason. I started asking about his access to local drives and the possibility that he Saved As in another location. Not only I was able to retrieve the file for him but funnily enough, I found a copy of it already opened on his laptop. Giggles.

On the same assignment, my boss Steve finally assigned me something to do. He presented himself with a huge dot matrix printer. Do you know those noisy, giant printers we used to put in server rooms because they were that loud and people complained about them all the time? Well, he wanted me to write a driver for it to connect to a brand-new Compaq computer. I had no idea where to start from. But it took me a minute to find that same printer on the list of upgraded items and what it would actually be upgraded to. A brand-new Compaq printer. I then wrote an email to him, explained the research I have done, and he was very impressed by the outcome. I remember attempting to write a printer driver before, when I worked with my father back in the day, in my beloved Genova. Tricky business, a lot of trial and error and in the end, we replaced the printer with a more modern one that worked immediately after attaching it to that 486 I had, from the Sabrina Salerno fan club deal. Lessons learned and a good few years later applied the same logic. Genius.

At the time when I was working for the Irish government and during my travels to give SQL training to the authorities, I found myself in the Dublin office. Several authorities' representatives had come to sit at my lecture which was an overall day between one thing and the other. In the morning, we would have more theoretical topics and after lunch, we would run real-life examples. Lunch was provided in the form of sandwiches and tea/coffee. During the break, I went around the room with a sandwich platter and asked everyone if they wanted to grab more. This lady from county Clare, in the beautiful West of Ireland, politely declines and adds, "If I do, I will need to shit on the train on my way back." Horror on many faces and I decided to respond, singing 'She is a lady' one of Tom Jones' most famous tunes. She probably still does not realise what she said that day!

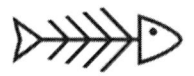

Back in the day when I was playing with Mad Poltergeist, if I weren't already in the rehearsal room at the back of the cemetery, Cristiano would collect me on his Mini Autobianchi and off we went to collect Franco, one of our guitar players. He was always late. Like hours late. One evening, we saw this cloud of smoke coming from the slope that Franco had to walk to reach the car, parked in a car park not too far from his apartment. It wasn't smoke. It was wood dust and Franco was completely covered in it strolling up the slope with his guitar. He got into the car and said, "I came straight from work (he was a carpenter at that time), and I did not have time for a shower…" I and Cristiano started laughing hysterically. Franco played all night still covered in that dust.

When I was playing in the band with no name with Aldo and Marco, we usually started at 1:00 am and finished around 3:00 am. Very long shifts as I explained in the book. One night, when I was back from a trip to Ireland to meet my beloved Jane, I invited them over to my apartment to try some of the Irish whiskeys I brought back from my journeys. They accepted even before I could finish the sentence. So, back at my place we were, sitting around my table in the kitchen and we started sampling from the three bottles that I had.

Sampling here, sampling there, it was not 4:00 am and we opened a second bottle. We opened the third bottle at around 5:00 am and we went through half of that before we decided to go around the block where there was a bakery that opened very early in the morning. We had hot pastries and croissants and then Aldo and Marco went straight to work! I think I just crawled back to my apartment and slept until 4:00 pm!

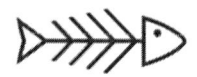

During my time playing in bands back in my beloved Genova, I often organised local concerts primarily with local bands. One famous night, in the middle of the coldest weather we had in Genova ever recorded, a friend of mine's band was up on stage. We invited the press, media and other people who were involved in keeping the city up to scratch with events and reviews. At the gates, one person presented himself. One. So, he paid for a ticket, entered the room, and sat in front of the stage, sipping a cocktail that he ordered from the bar. I recognised him, he was a reporter from Il Lavoro, a renowned newspaper in Genova. The band played anyway, I actually took the stage as well to sing a couple of covers, but in the stands, there was only one person who actually paid when he should not have. At the end of the night, we reimbursed the poor fella for the ticket and offered to pay for his drinks as well. In the next couple of days, my friend's band received the best review they ever had from a local newspaper.

Luca, who was playing the bass guitar that night, used to work for another local newspaper called Il Secolo XIX. He was approached by a prominent TV channel, with the intention to run a piece on the satanic cults active in Genova. To a price. He wasn't aware of any, so he decided to assemble a group of friends and make up one. Enzo was there, Claudio as the Black Priest, me as the guy screwing a sacrificial lady on the altar of damnation, two lovely ladies and a couple of others. The first thing we thought about was the dress code. So, we got some materials and quickly sewed up red costumes with golden inverted crosses on them, pointy hoods to disguise ourselves and we decided to go barefoot. We booked a rehearsal room in a place on the hills of Genova and made up the room with an altar, more crosses, a few skulls made of plastic really, and we agreed that we would consume beetroot to emulate a satanic communion. Or so the Black Priest said. He actually went out to gather information on these types of rituals and he did a great job at that. They were able to record on camera the ritual, a mix of Italian, Latin and gibberish really, but until the sacrifice part, so when the time came, I rolled my costume up, showing for the cameras my bare ass, and pretended to screw the lovely lady that was naked and placed on the altar of damnation. Luca who was the chaperone on the occasion, quickly let the camera crew out of the room and we closed the door behind them, pretending that the ritual and ceremony were still going. After the ceremony had concluded, I and Enzo posed again in front of the cameras to answer a few questions, rigorously in full costume attire, not to be recognised. The TV crowd was greeted away from Luca, he also got paid and the next thing I remember is all of us drinking cocktails in a bar in Piazza della Vittoria, and I came back home with two hundred thousand lire for my troubles. You better believe it.

A couple of years later, I was at the table having lunch with my parents and we had the TV on. The daily news hour. And all of a sudden, I see my bare ass on TV during the altar of damnation ritual! I quickly asked my mother the first question that came to mind, to distract her and get her attention off the news. A mother would know her son's bare ass!

Once during my radio days with Radio Magic Sound, I invited the band Hate (you remember them, do you?) for an interview. All four of them showed up accompanied by a large group of ladies (groupies?) to my surprise. Well, during the interview some were kissing, some were blowing, some were having sex and it started to get very late in the night. To my horror, Riccardo, the owner of the radio, was up that night listening to what was happening. He took his car and barged into the cubicle I was in. Fortunately, the room was quiet, and no sex or blowing was to be seen, bar a few records on the floor and a couple kissing passionately. So, he didn't make too much fuss and actually thanked me for being so late and keeping the radio and its fans entertained. Phew!

And last but not least, a parenthesis on a guy who is very important in my life, my brother Ricky. He is the hard worker in the family, always was and always will be. Like my father but not like me. Once on a call with my father, I said, "I am trained for nothing and I do nothing as a consequence."

And my father started to laugh very loudly and replied, "Well, at least you are honest." I miss him very much.

During my heavy metal days, my brother was always in the first row in the pit at my concerts. He gave me a lot of support despite the fact that there is a 7-year gap between the two of us, me, of course, being the eldest. His career has been quite hectic. After his diploma, he went and joined the army to then work for several years in an insurance company to then move to professional fisherman to then open his own company providing many types of services in his beloved Bonassola, close to Le Cinque Terre. He then closed the company and dedicated his time to look after gardens, look after buildings and all the work around them and is now a proud worker under il Comune di Bonassola. I love him dearly as my parents passed away a long time ago and he is literally all I got when it comes to family. He is married to Manuela, and they had a child they called Ariel. Ariel likes swimming, believe it or not. We now talk on WhatsApp, and we share passions for Panini Stickers, his Genoa and my Sampdoria, reminiscing the past and the good days with the parents and we talk about work as well and all his side projects. And mine.

He was instrumental in my upbringing and still is my dearest friend, the one I tell I got a new job, or I am on a plane to Florida and everything in between. He is actually going to be fifty soon and we are all going to Chiavari (where he lives with his family for a while now) to celebrate his birthday and life to date.

I cannot wait to see him again after this long pandemic.

Appendix III

To complement this story which I really thank you for having read till now, let me leave you with a few web links where you can find all my works and more.

Let's start with my YouTube channel where I keep everything related to my music experiences. Live, demos, albums, extras...

https://www.youtube.com/channel/UCuIiDp9bXtfWh5L2deNPfMQ

Also, you can find my music divided into colours (yes, I know...) on my official InduRancE website:

http://www.indurance.org

And finally, you can find all my other passions and hobbies including The Dark comics and a lot more on my collection database website:

http://www.irishspawn.com

I might as well give you also my Facebook page and my LinkedIn profile...

https://www.facebook.com/mcottica/

https://www.linkedin.com/in/maxcottica/

It was a great journey bringing you with me on this insane trip. A lot of memories, fortunately only a few regrets but writing a book has always been a dream of mine and now I ticked that box.

Upwards and onwards, onto the next project!